Toscani & Sons
Ristorante

Champagne & Sparkling Wines

	Vintage	Bottle
Mezza Corona Brut Reserva, Rotari (Italy)	1991	$29.00

Beautifully fresh focused and appealing featuring lots of lemony and spicy flavors, crisp acidity, and a tangy finish. Very youthful and elegant.

Glass

$8.00

Veuve Clicquot Brut (France) — 1989 — 65.00

Beautiful Toast and other complex aromas, with a clean lingering finish.

Louis Roederer Cristal (France)

Lush, rich and complex, from Champagnes most prestigious house. — 1989 — 150.00

Please note: All vintages are subject to change based upon the whims and capriciousness of life in general and are not to be viewed as a lack of concern on the part of the proprietor.

White Wines of Italy

	Vintage	Bottle
Pinot Grigio, La Colombaia (Valdadig) A light, dry, delicate taste is balanced by a clean refreshing finish.	1995	$18.00
Pinot Grigio, Santa Margherita (Dell'Alto Adige) Fine, delicate fruit, crisp and firm in structure with a slightly spicy nose.	1995	33.00
Pinot Grigio, Alois Lageder (Alto Adige) Refreshing, spicy and nutty.	1995	23.00
Pinot Grigio, Ecco Domani Floral nose with delicate aromas of fig and honeysuckle fruit, clean bold flavors, excellent balance and spicy finish.	1995	20.00
Pinot Grigio (Rose), Zeni (Trentino) Fermented on the skins for a short time to extract the rose color. Light and delicate, with aromas of apple and wild flowers.	1995	29.00
Orvieto Secco, Antinori (Umbria) Light - bodied, with floral aromas, very refreshing and enjoyable.	1995	17.00
Arneis, Accademia Torregiorgi (Piedmont) A fruity aroma with hints of pear, melon and pineapple, a full, round, agreeable, harmonious taste and a delicate, distinctive finish. Very elegant.	1995	26.00

White Wines of Italy

	Vintage	Bottle
Gaio, Rocca Di Fabbri (Umbria)	1995	$20.00
Crispy, dry, big in body, reminiscent of peaches, lemons and tropical fruit, Gaio's tiny <u>hint</u> of spritziness makes it memorable, unique and delicious.		
Aragosta, Vermentino Di Alghero (Sardina)	1995	19.00
A popular favorite, brimming with luscious flavors of lemony pineapples.		
Verdicchio Classico, Fazzi Battaglia (Marches)	1994	20.00
Crisp, dry, light but elegant aroma and flavor.		
Gavi, Valditerra (Piemont)	1995	31.00
Pungent grassy, green herbal, citric nose. Penetrating and juicy with excellent spearmint flavor.		
Chardonnay, Zeni (Trentino)	1995	29.00
Floral, cherry nose, with an intriguing vegetal complexity good texture and acidity gives the wine intensity and grip.		
Chardonnay "Cervaro Della Sala", Antinori (Umbria)	1994	50.00
Very fruity, rich, dry, complex, and elegant. French oak aged.		
Chardonnay "Carpineto", Farnito (Tuscany)	1995	33.00
Deliciously dry and refreshing.		
Chardonnay, Zamo' & Zamo' (Friuli)	1994	25.00
Crisp, bright fruit with lemon and apple character.		

White Wines of Italy

	Vintage	Bottle
Sauvignon Blanc, Farnetella (Tuscany)	1994	$39.00
Like a great sancerre but aged in wood. Bright, minerally yet delicate notes of gooseberry, sage and lemon.		
Bianco Di Marche "Fish Bottle", Opici (Marche)	1996	16.00
A light wine that is deliciously dry and refreshing.		
Greco Di Tufo, Feudi Di San Gregorio (Campania)	1995	25.00
Fruity bouquet with typical almond scent. Dry on the palate. Well balanced, fresh with a slightly bitter after-taste of almond.		

White Wines of the World

	Vintage	Bottle
Pinot Grigio, Long Vineyards (Napa Valley)	1995	$35.00
Full luscious apple - peach aromas with surprisingly rich flavors.		
Semillon/Chardonnay, Sokol Blosser (Oregon)	1995	16.00
This new wine combines the steely crisp herbal semillon with the softer, fruitier chardonnay resulting in a crisp dry wine.		
Viognier, "Mistral", Millbrook (New York)	1995	21.00
Full-bodied, dry white wine which exhibits flavors such as peaches and apricots and has a light aroma of spring flowers.		
Alchemy, Hidden Cellars (Mendocino)	1993	25.00
Blossomy, fruit-laden, rich, with a fascinating combination of pears, sweet oak and citrus. Blend of semillon and sauvignon blanc grapes.		
Fume' Blanc, Benzinger (Sonoma Valley)	1995	20.00
Classic sauvignon blanc with rich melon flavors, herbal notes and crisp, intense finish.		
Fume' Blanc "Alexander Valley", Iron Horse (Sonoma Valley)	1995	28.00
Floral, perfume-like qualities with a clean citrusy finish.		
Chenin Blanc Dry " Old Vines, Girard (Napa Valley)	1995	16.00
Fresh, lively wine, full of apple and melon flavors.		

White Wines of the World

	Vintage	Bottle
Chardonnay, Duck Walk (New York) A fetching appley bouquet, tropical fruit and cinnamon notes.	1995	$16.00
Chardonnay "Green Valley", Marimar (Sonoma Valley) Distinct for its spicy flavors, with layers of ripe pear, peach and smoky oak.	1994	35.00
Chardonnay "Chalkhill", Chalk Hill Estate (Sonoma Valley) Richly textured, with tropical and apple flavors which are lush, ripe and complex.	1994	39.00
Chardonnay "Vintners Blend, "Ravenswood (Sonma Valley) A bright, lively wine with scents of apple, pears and peaches.	1995	23.00
Chardonnay "Monterey", Raymond (Central Coast) Distinctive grassy edge to the grapefruit and citrus flavors, graced by pear and spice notes.	1994	21.00
White Zinfandel, Beringer (Napa Valley) Soft, blush-colored, fresh berry flavors, dry finish.	1996	15.00

Red Wines of Italy

	Vintage	Bottle
Merlot, La Prendina (Lombardy)	1994	$24.00
Light to medium body with elegant black cherry, anise and cedar notes. Beautiful berry aromas that lead to a spicy finish.		
Montepulciano D'Abruzzo, Colle Secco Tollo (Abruzzi)	1995	17.00
Deep aromas of char and herbs; rich and thick on the palate, with a supple texture.		
Montepulciano D'Abruzzo, Farnese (Abruzzi)	1995	16.00
Bright and intense berry fruits, ruby red with violet tints, well balanced, with soft tannins.		
Montepulciano D'Abruzzo, Zaccagnini (Abruzzi)	1995	23.00
A distinct nose of plums, pepper and chocolate leads into a wine that is supple yet spicy , almost wiry in the mouth.		
Sangiovese "Dell 'Umbria", Rocco DiFabbri (Umbria)	1993	18.00
A rough 'n ready red, bursting with ripe aromas and flavors of earthy, raisiny cherries and plums.		
Sangiovese, Fontella (Marche)	1994	18.00
Light bodied and fruity, with stylishly supple cherry flavors, and excellent balance of freshness and complexity on the palate.		
Pinot Nero, Sant Elena Isonza (Friuli)	1994	25.00
Nuances of red currants, plum and oak. Well balanced with texture and sweetness.		

Red Wines of Italy

	Vintage	Bottle
Vvalpolicella Classico, Brigaldara (Veneto) An elegant, medium-bodied wine with a flavor of bitter cherries and bright young fruit.	1995	19.00
Valpolicella Classico Superiore, Zenato (Veneto) Full-flavored, dark and extracted . Plumy, red fruits in the nose, round and lush.	1993	16.00
Chianti, Campobello (Tuscany) Violet and strawberry nose, a dry, fruity harmonious taste and a pleasant finish.	1995	16.00
Chianti Classico Riserva, Antinori (Tuscany) Deep ruby-red, violet and vanilla bouquet; medium -bodied. Rich in extracts and tannins yet balanced, soft and stylish, with a fine lingering finish.	1993	32.00
Chianti Classico Riserva Ducale Gold, Ruffino (Tuscany) Exquisitely dry taste which has acquired a generous nobility and distinguished fineness from its selected origin and particularly careful aging.	1988	57.00
Chianti Classico Riserva, Casaloste (Tuscany) Organically grown grapes. Complex aromas and flavors of earthy cherries and raspberries, backed by lush nuances of French oak.	1993	31.00
Chianti Classico "Tenuta Santedame", Ruffino (Tuscany) Distinct structure, ruby red in color, with an intense bouquet and an elegant, notable character in the taste.	1993	26.00

Red Wines of Italy

	Vintage	Bottle
Rosso Di Montalciano, Tenuta Friggiali (Tuscany) Intense, medium ruby color with pronounced spicy oak and astonishing notes of blackberry and cherry.	1994	$30.00
Rosso Di Montalcino "Centine", Castello Banfi (Tuscany) Soft, fruity, full taste with spicy notes.	1994	18.00
Brunello, Di Montalcino Riserva, Aleramici (Tuscany) Intense ruby to bright, garnet , dry and warm in flavor, lightly tannic with great structure and aromatic length.	1991	49.00
Brunello Di Montalcino, Col D'orcia (Tuscany) Rather traditional in style, this shows chestnut and berry notes on the nose and palate, light tannins and a fresh finish.	1991	58.00
Canneto D'Angelo, (Basilicata) An intense bouquet, ample and ethereal, a full, taste, harmonious and smooth.	1991	38.00
Brusco Dei Barbi, Francesca Colombini (Tuscany) A medium-bodied wine with loads of fresh raspberry, cherry and blackberry flavors and soft tannins.	1994	20.00
Barolo, Cappellano (Piedmont) Rich, full, round expression of nebbiolo fruit, black cherry and smoked licorice flavors.	1991	48.00

Red Wines of Italy

	Vintage	Bottle
Barolo "Estate Bottlled", Franco Cesari (Piedmont) Dry, full, balanced velvety deep scent of violets and faded roses.	1991	$51.00
Barolo, Pio Cesare (Piedmont) Medium - bodied, well rounded and smooth, good fruit flavors and a nice woodsy aroma.	1992	57.00
Cabernet Sauvignon "Farnito", Carpineto (Tuscany) A full rich, elegant taste with nuances of blueberries and a lingering finish.	1993	36.00
Cabernet Sauvignon "Vigneto Del Falcone" LaPrendina (Lombardy) Fresh black fruit aromas accented by pine, eucalyptus and mint, with velvety texture, exquisite balance, and a very long finish.	1993	33.00
Amarone, La Colombaia (Veneto) A powerful, distinctive taste, fruity in its youth and austere as it ages. Soft lingering finish.	1990	36.00
Amarone Classico, Allegrini (Veneto) Deep blackberry, almond and chestnut aromas, smooth rich fruit with deep concentrated flavors.	1990	59.00
Amarone Della Valpolicella Classico, Luigi Righetti, (Veneto) Combines power and complexity in a full-bodied style. It ingrates spicy, earthy aromas with ripe, deep cherry and raisin flavors culminating in a long, lingering very dry finish.	1990	45.00

Red Wines of the World

	Vintage	Bottle
Merlot, Hogue Cellars (Washington)	1994	32.00
Rich and intense berry-like aroma which is enhanced by aging in small oak barrels. The flowers are soft, clean and smooth.		
Merlot, Markham (Napa Valley)	1994	32.00
Berry and cherry aromas with a subtle touch of oak. Soft, silky textures unfold on the palate with a round tannin.		
Pinot Noir, King Estate, (Oregon)	1994	33.00
Deep black cherry, raspberry aromas enhanced by hints of ciders, cinnamon and black pepper integrated with sweet oak and vanilla. A long spicy finish.		
Meritage "Mythology", Pindar (New York)	1993	40.00
A complex, dry red with a full-body, robust, with toasted oak and black cherry and cassis flavors.		
Cabernet Sauvignon, Chateau Souverain (Sonoma Valley)	1993	26.00
Rich, concentrated flavors of currant, blackberry and coffee balanced by soft tannins and vanilla, oak nuances.		
Cabernet Sauvignon, Freemark Abbey (Napa Valley)	1989	44.00
Rich, ruby, medium-bodied. Balanced acidity, moderately extracted and oaked.		
Cabernet Sauvignon, Simi (Sonoma Valley)	1993	35.00
Fresh and vibrant, complex and concentrated, fresh cherry, currant, plum and berry flavors.		
Cabernet Sauvignon Reserve, Raymond (Napa Valley)	1994	33.00
Medium-bodied , pleasantly balanced cabernet with spicy berry, black currant, plum, and Tobacco flavors. Showing aromas of blackberry with earthy, dusty notes and hints of licorice/anise, the nose is complex and exciting.		

Red Wines of the World

	Vintage	Bottle
Cabernet Sauvignon, Livingston (Napa Valley)	1994	$35.00

Bright bouquet of black cherries, currants, licorice, lavender, plum, cinnamon and minerals. On the palate, the flavors of black pit fruits, layered berries, clove, anise and tarragon are balanced and focused, with good depth and a fruity, spicy finish with moderate tannins.

	Vintage	Bottle
Cabernet Franc "Imagery", Benziger (Sonoma Valley)	1994	33.00

Deep, rich, concentrated blackberry flavors with a long persistent finish.

	Vintage	Bottle
Cabernet Franc, Chateau Ste Michelle (Washington)	1993	42.00

Dry, robust flavor, mellowed by aging in oak barrels.

	Vintage	Bottle
Zinfandel "Jack London", Kenwood (Sonoma Valley)	1994	36.00

Rich and complex, well balanced, intense, berry and pepper flavors, has a long smooth finish.

NICHOLAS FAITH

CHÂTEAU
MARGAUX

PHOTOGRAPHS
MICHEL GUILLARD

THE VENDOME PRESS

in association with
CHRISTIE'S WINE PUBLICATIONS

Château Margaux
by Nicholas Faith

Original edition published in 1980 by Christie's Wine Publications

This revised edition first published in the United Kingdom in 1991 by

Mitchell Beazley Publishers
Artist's House
14-15 Manette Street
London W1VB 5LB

Published in the United States of America and Canada by

The Vendome Press
515 Madison Avenue
New York, NY 10022

Distributed in the USA and Canada by
Rizzoli International Publications
300 Park Avenue South
New York, NY 10010

©Flammarion 1988, Text © 1980, 1991 Nicholas Faith

LIBRARY OF CONGRESS
Library of Congress Cataloging-in-Publication Data

Faith, Nicholas, 1933-
[Château Margaux. English]
Château Margaux/by Nicholas Faith.
p. cm.
Translation of: Château Margaux.
Includes index.
ISBN 0-86565-106-X : $50.00
1. Château Margaux (Firm) 2. Wine and wine making – France – Margaux. I. Title.
TP553.F3313 1988
338.7'61663'2230–dc19
88-17152
CIP

Editor: Jane Eaton, Elizabeth Bellord
Typesetting: Kerri Hinchon
Production of text film: Ted Timberlake
Senior Executive Editor: Christopher Foulkes

Text film by Mitchell Beazley in 10/10½ point Garamond book, and 9/9½ point Garamond Italic
Printed and bound in France.

First page: *A case-end from Château Margaux.*
Previous double page: *Sphinxes at the base of the steps leading up to the château.*

CONTENTS

Plan
du Domaine
DE CHATEAU MARGAUX
Appartenant à
monsieur le MARQUIS
DE LA COLONILLA

Echelle du pieds d'atacheur

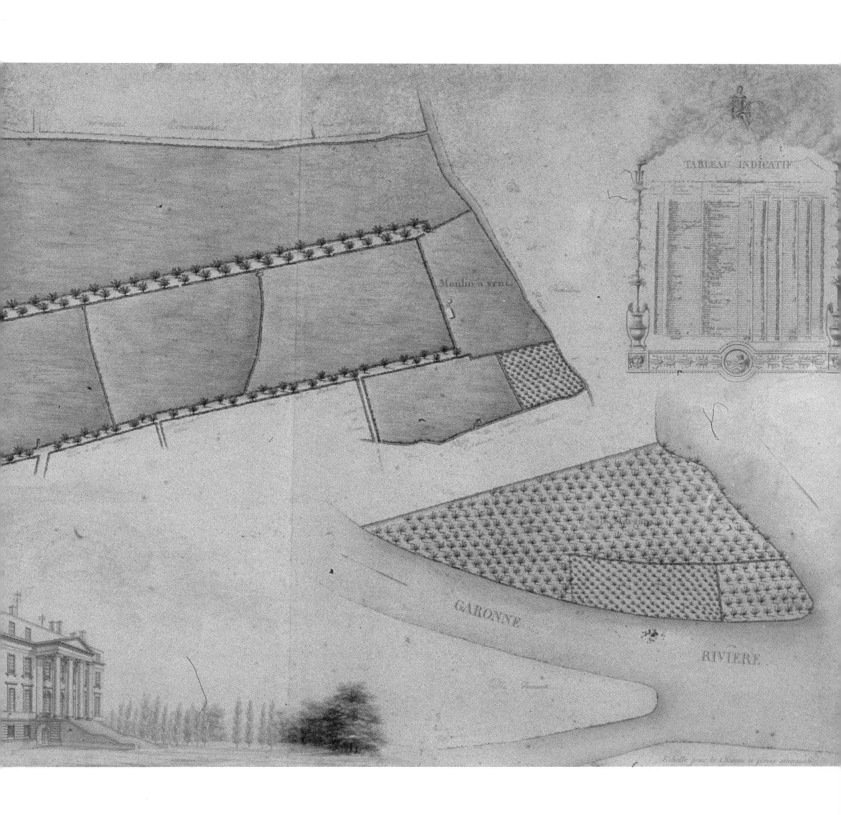

TABLEAU INDICATIF

Moulin a vent

GARONNE

RIVIERE

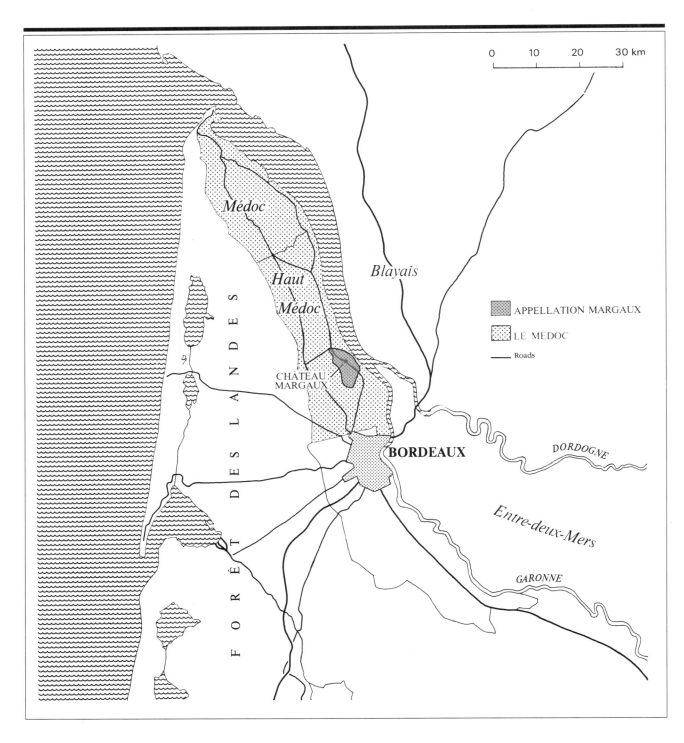

Médoc

*Haut
Médoc*

Blayais

APPELLATION MARGAUX

LE MÉDOC

Roads

CHÂTEAU
MARGAUX

F O R Ê T   D E S   L A N D E S

BORDEAUX

DORDOGNE

Entre-deux-Mers

GARONNE

0   10   20   30 km

*Château Margaux and the Margaux appellation in the
Médoc.*

INTRODUCTION

THE UNIQUENESS OF MARGAUX

The road out of Margaux turns sharply left as it leaves the straggling, undistinguished village on its way north to St-Julien and Pauillac. Ahead at the corner lies a typical slope of the carefully trimmed vines growing on poor, pebbly soil which make up virtually the whole landscape around the village. To the right is a lane leading down to the river Gironde a mile away. And to the right again is a high stone wall, built by the owners of Château Margaux in the nineteenth century to prevent passers-by from seeing down the hill to their magnificent château and its park. But the gate set into the doorway at the corner of the wall is generally open and within can be seen – not the château itself, for this is hidden in the trees – but more vines within a sloping enclosure leading down to a stream.

These parcels of land are only part of the estate: but without them Margaux would be merely one of the anonymous thousands of so-called "châteaux" which litter the whole départment of the Gironde. For they are the heart of the château's vineyard; it is they which underpin the quality of the carefully assembled blend of wines from different parts of the estate which together are sold as Château Margaux. Today, Professor Emile Peynaud, Bordeaux's most distinguished oenologist, who is now the chief adviser to the château, reckons that, "the walled vineyard behind the park is the heart of the quality of the château".

But the ensemble, the totality we call Château Margaux, depends on more than a couple of well-placed, curiously constituted fields. The emergence and survival of the name as synonymous with fine wine have also depended on the existence of an estate large enough to support a long-term investment in the vineyard and in the ageing of its wine. You may not be able to see the château from the most productive parts of the estate, but the fortunes of the two are inseparable; only the estate had the resources to exploit the qualities of the wines which the stony earth was capable of producing. The estate would not have been famous without the wines, but the earth needed an owner with the money, the long-term view, the intolerance and the meticulous long-term standards which alone could ensure its fame.

Fortunately for Margaux, it has, at crucial periods in its history, possessed such owners. And that is why it presents today such an "aristocratic" appearance, regular fields with a hierarchy of roads, cart-tracks and paths. It is by no accident that "the Médocain châteaux, and especially the

Barriques in the main chai: "the Temple of Wine".

crus classés, can be numbered among the very biggest French landed estates" in the words of one author. Over the past three centuries, the estate has varied in size, but it has generally comprised over 600 acres in the commune of Margaux, as well as extensive holdings in neighbouring villages. Moreover, Château Margaux, situated just where the vine-bearing banks of gravel start to emerge from the alluvium of the riverside meadows, has always been the best-balanced agricultural estate among the leading growths in the Gironde.

So the history of the estate during the three centuries since the wine first emerged from the anonymous mass of clarets is of central importance. Inevitably, with so many owners, their relations with the estate varied widely. But they were all, in the final analysis, the guardians of the "brand" name Margaux, so they played a crucial role – even if it was sometimes a negative one – in determining the quality of the wine. If, as sometimes happened, they wanted a quick return on their money, then the estate would over-produce. If they were not interested in the estate, or had grown old and therefore careless, or simply did not have adequate financial resources to

The sloping roofs of the main façade. Magnolias and camelias were planted en masse to lend an air of informality to the gardens (above).
The first view of the château is through an impressive avenue of plane trees. The driveway was formerly referred to as the chemin royal (right).

invest, then again, quality suffered. Of course they did not actually make the wine, the role of the key men who have run estates like Margaux through the centuries – the estate manager (*régisseur*), the cellarmaster (*maître de chai*) and the *chef de culture* in charge of the vines themselves – has always been crucial and has usually been under-estimated. Nevertheless they worked within a framework, and whatever their quality (and they have included some notable figures) they could never entirely compensate for their employers' inadequacies. For some of the owners, especially during the nineteenth century, Margaux was merely one of a number of estates, bought or kept because it was the right thing to do to own a major *cru classé,* just as it might be to keep a string of racehorses (or a leading *danseuse* from the Opera). But fortunately for the good name of Margaux, the estate was a visceral passion for some owners, a crucial element in their life, and it is their tenures which have to be analysed with the greatest attention. Inevitably, I have devoted a great deal of space to the fortunes of the château, the wine and the estate since the end of 1976. The purchase of Margaux by the Greek-born financier, André Mentzelopoulos, inaugurated one of the most remarkable periods in the history, not only of Margaux, but of its peers. Within a couple of years Margaux's unique *terroir* (soil) had been freed, was able to shout out loud, allowing the wine to jump in one bound from being "last of the firsts" to, in that felicitous old phrase, "the best-succeeded wine of the year", a status it has maintained in the majority of the vintages ever since.

The transformation in the wine has been echoed by the multitude of changes in the estate, the vineyard, and the château itself, changes all conducted with a great deal of money and, far more importantly, an equal dose of flair and determination to remain faithful to the original. But the happiest aspect of the story since 1976 has been the love affair between the château and the Mentzelopoulos family, an unlikely alliance which has descended from father to daughter and may even extend to the third generation.

The Mentzelopoulos' are fully aware that they are guardians, not just of a handful of gravel slopes but of an aristocratic tradition and a physical setting, which owes much to one of their more extraordinary predecessors, Bertran Douat, Marquis de la Colonilla. For him, returning home after making his fortune – and buying his title – in Spain was a triumph to be celebrated with a building worthy of its owner's feelings. For the other element in any work on Margaux must be the château itself: although known as the "Versailles of the Médoc" the soubriquet is misleading. It is, rather, a medium-sized country house set in the centre of its estate and thus seen to its best advantage in a rural setting of gravel and lawns, massed trees and bushes, an informal moat and a formal avenue, as a celebration of the qualities of the estate's wine.

The combination of elements summed up in the words "Château Margaux" – the wine, the *terroir* and its setting, the estate and the château itself – is unique, even in the Médoc among Margaux`s peers as "first-growth clarets". But for a number of reasons no history of the estate can be as thorough or as authoritative as the recent work by a team of French academics on Château Latour. At Margaux, the constant succession of changing owners has precluded any continuity in the records.

Moreover, because successive owners attached very different importance to their possession, outside documents illuminate the story of the estate only in flashes. Fortunately one of these provides us with a full account of the estate during the most crucial and troubled times in its history, during the French Revolution. For the original edition of this book, written for Christie's Wine Publications in 1980, I was lucky to be able to refer to the massive thesis on the wines of the Médoc written by M. Réne Pijassou. I was also able to rely, as can any serious researcher, on the fact that the "community of claret" – merchants, brokers and growers alike – is both infinitely patient and historically minded. The previous owners of the estate, Pierre and Bernard Ginestet, contributed enormously to the original book, as did André and Laura Mentzelopoulos.

Their daughter Corinne and her *régisseur,* Paul Pontallier, were towers of helpfulness and good sense when I was given the opportunity of bringing the book up-to-date. And I have been able to expand and restore some sections of the book thanks to the confidence of Chris Foulkes, and the patience and professional skills of Jane Eaton.

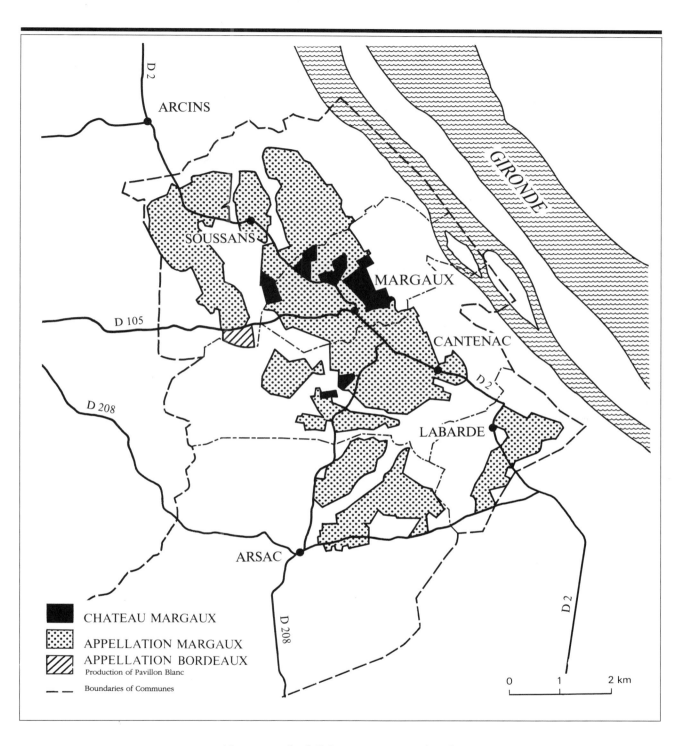

ARCINS

D 2

SOUSSANS

MARGAUX

GIRONDE

D 105

CANTENAC

D 2

D 208

LABARDE

ARSAC

D 208

D 2

CHATEAU MARGAUX

APPELLATION MARGAUX

APPELLATION BORDEAUX
Production of Pavillon Blanc

Boundaries of Communes

0   1   2 km

*The vineyards of Château Margaux within the
Margaux appellation. Château Margaux is the only
Grand Cru Classé in Bordeaux to bear the same name
as its appellation (above).*

THE
FORTUNES OF
MARGAUX

Margaux has, for several hundred years, resembled more or less closely a *beau idéal,* not only of claret, but also of a country estate. In the words of Paul de Cassagnac (translated by Guy Knowles): "It forms a complete agricultural property, self-sufficing in everything."

Cassagnac's description of the estate dates only from the 1930s, but its size and shape were beginning to be recognizable at the end of the sixteenth century, and by 1700 had largely assumed the form we know today. And this is totally different from any other in the Médoc. To be sure, many major properties were adorned by distinguished houses long before the present Château Margaux was built in the first decade of the nineteenth century but none had the balance of Margaux. Regrettably, the attractions of the estate have been rather overshadowed by the majesty of the present house. Yet, even before the French Revolution, when the then château was a far less imposing affair, the estate was a distinguished one.

Its boundaries stretched – as they still do – from the main road from Bordeaux to Pauillac down to the river, and the English visitor finds many echoes of his own landscape. Although Palladio was not an Englishman, country houses employing his ideas are far more general a feature of the English than the French landscape. One familiar feature is the dependence of the village church on the manor house. For the property is not in the centre of the village, but lies at the south-east corner of the commune. Also familiar to an English eye is the mixture of formality and informality, of agricultural practicality and aristocratic landscaping, which characterizes the whole estate. The actual house is dignity itself – there is a formal avenue leading down to the river, and the approach is regular, but there is a tell-tale sign of informality in the sprawling but magnificent magnolia tree to the left of the château, in front of the beechwoods. The château's formality and dignity stand out the more effectively because it is surrounded by vines, by informal woods and gardens, and by a major agricultural business. It can never be a hollow historical monument:

rather it is the living symbol of the power and prosperity of a major agricultural estate, and of the quality of its wine.

Not that the property is, or ever was, exclusively viticultural. Vines have, traditionally, occupied only a third of its five or six hundred acres – and even then they were not continuous. They were interrupted by the land and buildings of Château Abel Laurent (which was combined with Margaux only after World War II) and by the incursions of other châteaux – Malescot St Exupéry's vines stretch right down to the stream at the foot of Cap de Haut. Moreover, even among the alien vines there are touches of a rather English aristocratic whimsy: two of the wells, at the boundary between Margaux's land and Malescot's, were covered during the nineteenth century with classical cupolas. One of these forms the focus for the path through the trees leading from the château,

The wrought iron gate at the entrance to the château (above).
Aerial views of the château show how the estate stretches down toward the Gironde (above left) and, at closer quarters how extensive restoration work has preserved it as a historic monument (below left).

and both lend an air of fantasy to that side of the vineyard.

The spirit of fantasy is also expressed on the other side of the château in what an anonymous English traveller once described as "an old shepherd's hut, that looks as if it had been imported from Italy, so closely does it resemble the buildings of Tuscany or Latium", a building that used to stand in the meadows beyond the park. Nearer the house is the "moat" between the garden and the meadows stretching down to the river. This is strictly a landscapist's image, never intended for military use. But it does serve a purpose. Seen in conjunction with the château it is undeniably picturesque, and breaks the view between the garden and the meadows. Over 50 acres of the pasture form Le Grand Barrail between the house and the river, long an integral part of the property. The meadows fulfil an important agricultural purpose. In the summer they feed the cattle which in their winter quarters provide the vines with the manure they need.

Unfortunately the only pictorially inadequate element is the river itself. The Gironde is generally both wide and sluggish. In this stretch it has formed a number of islands. A couple of these (including the Ile d'Issan – nearly 80 acres of meadow, marsh and wood) have historically been part of the estate: they are virtually part of the river bank, and separated only by easily-bridged streams. Moreover, because of the presence of these "islands", the area between *Le Grand Barrail* and the river is by no means beautiful. There are straggly woods and rather marshy meadows, and the site of a couple of mills, and the remains of the two little landing-places in the commune, again, traditionally part of the estate itself. But the mixtures of the mud flats and islands ensured that there could never be any great depth of water, and they have been steadily silting up in the course of the past couple of hundred years.

Even before the little "ports" silted up, they were not of any importance; and their insignificance was decisive in ensuring that Margaux was relatively insignificant, either as estate or lordship, until the vine conquered the Médoc. But that was not until the late sixteenth and above all the seventeenth century. Before that the peninsula was largely *friches,* poor scrubland, with meagre crops, mostly of rye, tended by impoverished peasants owing allegiance usually to insignificant lords. Because there were no roads up the Médoc the river was virtually the only means of transport and communication; especially for the English kings who ruled the whole of Aquitaine for nearly 300 years, and for their subjects who imported enormous quantities of wine from Bordeaux for several centuries.

This neglect of the Médoc continued during the first century of the French re-occupation of Bordeaux. Once they had recovered from the shock, the burghers of Bordeaux started to buy up estates around about the city, and to cultivate vines there. They were led by the *Parlementaires* – the families which until the French Revolution dominated the local Parlement. But for a long time the *parlementaires* concentrated their efforts on the "Graves" just south of the city (it was by no accident that the first claret to be individually famous, Haut-Brion, came from an estate now enfolded within the city's southern suburbs). Moreover, the jealousy of the Bordeaux merchants had blocked any development to the north for a long time: to preserve their monopoly of the English wine trade, they prevented ships from the ports between Bordeaux and the sea from indulging in foreign trade. All this started to change in the late sixteenth century.

Before that date the history of Margaux is obscure. There are legends and myths and a not very reliable list of seigneurs of *"La Mothe Margaux",* who were vassals of the Châtellerie of Blanquefort, strategically located near Bordeaux astride the bridge over the vital *jalle de Blanquefort.* It is possible that the King of England, as Duke of Aquitaine, owned the seigneurie for some time. It is possible, too, that some English sailors landed at Margaux in the last decade of the fourteenth century and pillaged the vineyard.

But despite its relative unimportance, Margaux had already numbered some well-known families among its seigneurs before the sixteenth century. The d'Albrets were the seigneurs when the first records appeared in the middle of the thirteenth century. It passed by marriage to the Montferrands – *Messire François de Montferrand, Premier Baron de Guienne,* who was named *Sieur de la terre de Margaux* in a deed dated 1447. When he

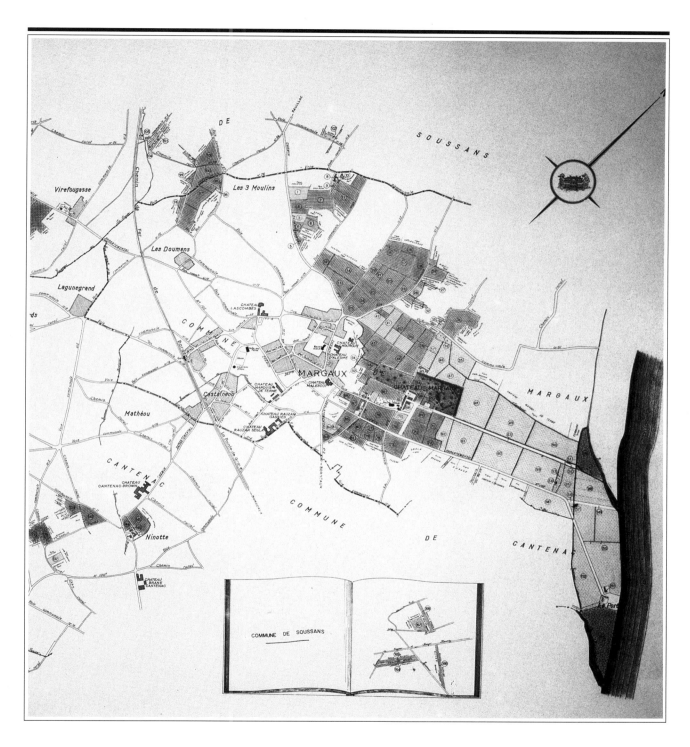

*Official land survey of the existing domaine, registered
in 1986, showing the vast number of parcels of land.*

*The parcel of land known as Le Cuvier borders directly
on to the château and chai (above). The parish church
of St-Michel is surrounded by vines (below).*

was exiled after the French re-conquest a few years later, the estate passed to Thomas de Durfort, of the family still celebrated by the vineyard of Durfort-Vivens, on the other side of the road from Margaux itself. The first incursion of capital from Bordeaux into Margaux arrived when Jean Gimel, a famous merchant, bought the *seigneuries* from Thomas de Durfort in 1480. On his death 11 years later it passed to the Lory taining the value and quality of a property and its wine lies in continuity, and for over two centuries following the arrival of the Lestonnacs, the estate was, effectively, in one family. The names changed, to d'Aulède, to Fumel, to d'Hargicourt, but only because the property passed through the female line on three occasions. It was only in the first decade of the nineteenth century that the last Fumel, the redoubtable Laure, eventually sold the

family, into which his daughter had married.

The shaping of the property as we know it today was the work of the Lestonnac family. They first came on the scene in Margaux in the last quarter of the sixteenth century. The Margaux estate was lucky. For the crucial element in main- estate. Margaux was also lucky: all these families were distinguished, and one of them contracted a marriage which virtually ensured Margaux's place as a wine of importance. Before individual châteaux emerged as "brand names", the Lestonnacs did much of the reorganization in the

L'allée du presbytère, which leads from the church to the main driveway.

*Plan of Chateau Margaux as represented on a scrolled
map of the Gironde, dating from 1759.*

late sixteenth century. In no fewer than 40 land transactions between 1572 and 1584, recorded in documents still preserved at the château, *"L'honorable homme, Pierre de Lestonnac, jurat de la présente ville de Bordeaux"* (Pierre de Lestonnac, gentleman, alderman of Bordeaux) bought, largely from the local peasantry, dozens of plots of land, either in the heart of the estate (particularly on the Puch Sem Peyre) or nearby, in return for the plots the family had inherited in the surrounding communes. The steady reshaping of their land by the Lestonnacs is a classic example of a process which was to take place – albeit rather later – all over the Médoc where, previously, the land had been tilled in small disjointed plots by the peasants for grain, within a century whole communes, and none more so than Margaux, were dominated by a few vineyards. Moreover, the conquest of the Médoc by capital from Bordeaux brought with it a parallel revolution, the direct exploitation of their land by the purchasers, and, where the land was suitable, exclusively for vines.

Although there may well have been vines on the slopes of *La Mothe Margaux* in the late fourteenth century (hence the story of the English sailors), even in the third quarter of the sixteenth century the size of the tithe, *la dime et le dimen,* payable to the Rector (*Curé*) of Blanquefort, shows that the estate produced only a sixth as much wine in the fourteenth as in the eighteenth century. But this meagre production was before the arrival of the Lestonnacs who were operating on an altogether larger scale than their predecessors. Unluckily for them, they had joined a revolt in Bordeaux in the early sixteenth century against excessive royal taxation. The head of the family was executed when the rebellion was suppressed, and they did not regain their previous importance until the Fronde.

The estate went to the son of another sister, Françoise, who had married into an even more distinguished family, the d'Aulèdes, who had arrived in Aquitaine as early as the ninth century. It was Jean, from the senior branch of the family, who married Françoise de Lestonnac in 1582. To inherit his uncle's estates on his death in 1612, their son Pierre had to take his name, to become "Pierre d'Aulède de Lestonnac". But the Château of Margaux was occupied for most of the first half of the century by his sister, Olive de Lestonnac. She died in 1648, and her brother five years later, and the estate passed to his son, Jean-Denis d'Aulède de Lestonnac.

THE PONTACS AND THE ENGLISH

The estate inherited by Jean-Denis d'Aulède was already a fine one. A *terrier,* or land register, drawn up by two notaries in the 1680s shows clearly how successful the family had been in consolidating its holdings, and then in building up their production of wine. The estate covered about 650 acres, which has probably been its average size ever since. Significantly, under a third was let off to a great many small tenants who were by no means exclusively devoted to viticulture. Neither, of course, was the domaine itself: both tenants and lord used around 44 per cent of their holdings for growing grapes; but whereas the peasants were occupying small holdings, the lord, with 470 acres under his direct control, could devote 188 of them to vines – much the same as today's figures – and still have a balanced estate.

In 1654 the marriage was contracted between Jean-Denis and Thérèse de Pontac. The Pontacs were probably Bordeaux's leading upper-middle-class family, and one which played an absolutely crucial role in the history of the wines of Bordeaux. Thérèse's father was *Premier Président* of Bordeaux's *Parlement.* This post he bequeathed to his son- in-law, Jean-Denis.

His tenure of the post was a troubled one. Three years after he had taken over as *Premier Président* the Bordelais rioted against heavy taxation and monopolies, forcing *Parlement* to be hastily evacuated. It only returned fourteen years later. In the meantime, d'Aulède's father-in-law had died and thus opened the way for lengthy and costly family arguments over inheritance rights.

Eventually Madame d'Aulède acquired a half-share in the major and historic family property at Haut-Brion, in the Graves just south of Bordeaux (as well as a major estate, Château de Pez, in St-Estèphe). At Haut-Brion, Arnaud de Pontac had created the model for all subsequent major wine-growing estates. The first mention of a named

Following double page: The main entrance hall strikes a note that is manifest throughout the château – one of restrained grandeur and elegance.

claret is of Haut-Brion (in Pepys's diary), for Pontac had close connections with the "café society" of Restoration London; he numbered the diarist Evelyn among his friends, and his son opened a smart coffee house under the family name.

The idea that one bottle of claret could be distinguished from another was a revolutionary one, although the English had been the major consumers of Bordeaux wines for 400 years or more, and had even adapted the old French word *clairet* (meaning a pale, almost rosé-like wine) to describe it. But it took the fashion-consciousness of the hedonistic, very public society of Restoration London, a centre of truly conspicuous consumption, combined with the desire of the Pontacs to provide rather more carefully made and selected wine, to give birth to the idea of a "branded" claret. At first the wines had relied on the name of the family more even than on their geographical origin: "Pontack" was as powerfully evocative of good wine as "Haut-Brion". Naturally the d'Aulèdes, owning another major estate as well as Haut-Brion, were well-placed to take advantage of the new market.

Curiously the wars between England and France during most of the formative years of the new brands did not cripple their development. However, the Pontacs and their relations did experience a short period of anxiety in the mid-1690s when, due to bad weather, four successive vintages were almost totally lost. Moreover, for the first time, the British and the Dutch were allied against the

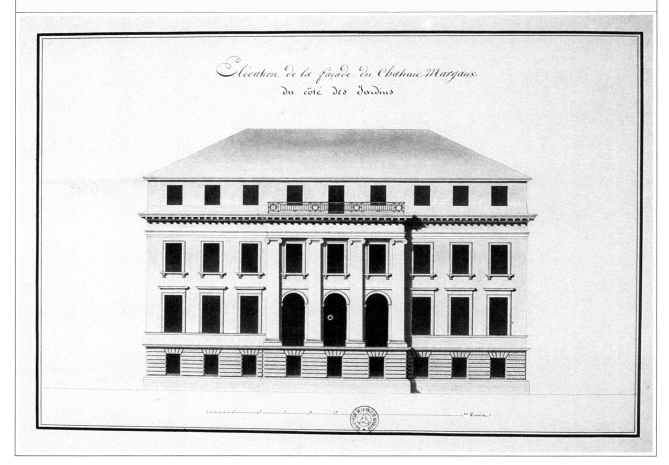

Louis Combes' design for the northern façade. This was not the final solution, although it corresponds to the present building in many ways.

French and successfully imposed a blockade of the French coast.

In theory, then, the War of the Spanish Succession, which broke out in 1702 after a mere four-year lull, should have spelled the end for the idea that better clarets could be sold on the English market. Instead it marked the beginning of a mutual dependence between Bordeaux's wines and English drinkers which lasted two and a half centuries and ended only when other nationalities (notably the Americans) began to buy claret on a large scale in the years after World War II.

For the English aristocracy managed to acquire their claret even in war-time. With suspicious frequency French ships carrying loads of choice vintages were captured, the cargoes put up for auction in the City of London, and the sales advertised in the *London Gazette*. There were over 150 such auctions in the eight years before 1711, when the blockade was effectively lifted and more regular trade could be resumed.

The name "Margaux" (in varying spellings) crops up repeatedly in the course of these sales. Moreover it is one of only four names which do recur: the others, not surprisingly, being those of Lafite, Latour and Haut-Brion. This was often still referred to as Pontac. After 1707, another key word crept in to the announcements. On 22nd May that year, the London Gazette advertised: "New French Prize Clarets... being of the growths (*crus*) of Lafitt, Margouze and Latour". Significant is the first use of the word "growth", which has not been absent from the Bordeaux wine business since then. And with the identification of individual clarets came an insistence on their authenticity.

Within a few years after the relaxation of the blockade the growing number of named growths, and indeed wines from a specific commune, began to fetch prices decidedly higher than those obtained by anonymous clarets. Moreover production was expanding rapidly. The great frost of early 1709, which caused considerable suffering, led to a tightening up of the regulations designed to prevent the expansion of the area devoted to the vine as opposed to the grain. These were designed to counteract the *fureur de planter* ("planting madness"), as the craze to plant more vines was described by contemporaries.

As early as 1714, a Parisian wine merchant writ-

ing to his correspondent in Bordeaux talks of "the good and excellent wines of Bordeaux, old, deep-coloured and velvety". His agent was instructed to put it in bottles "protected by wicker" and "well-stoppered with corks and duly sealed with wax" before despatching them to London. The whole set of instructions is full of significant new words. Where previously claret had been anonymous, it now came from "Margaux", a defined château (or commune). Where previously it was considered a light wine from the latest vintage, here it is a dark wine being sent to London "in little cases, each holding fifty bottles in the Italian fashion", each bottled, corked and sealed with wax.

These precautions were financially well worth-while. The 1714 shipment included some "Pontac"

The façade that was actually carried through in 1810. The final design has central pilasters in front of which is a wide terrace. From this a double flight of steps sweeps down in a horseshoe-shape to the garden.

Fine lengths of willow, called vimes, (above: top left and bottom right) gathered from the estate's own osiery (below right) are traditionally employed to bind the vines. Wooden stakes (above: top right and bottom left) support the vines and hold the training wires in place (above right).

worth virtually double the price fetched by ordinary "Graves", and the other three growths also commanded a substantial premium, which more than compensated for the relatively small quantities being shipped to Britain even after the war formally ended in 1713.

The predominance of the Big Four is clear from the purchasing habits of a select few of the English upper classes. Either Haut-Brion or, sometimes Lafite, seemed to hold the premier position, but the other two were always only a few per cent below the others and could sometimes even command a premium over them.

The most famous claret buyer in the early years was Sir Robert Walpole, who was the first British Prime Minister to depend on Parliament rather than on the whims of the sovereign. Like so many of his kind before and since, he used alcohol lavishly to lubricate his manoeuvres. Only, instead of the "Bourbon and branchwater" employed to woo American senators and congressmen, he used his favourite wines, Lafite and Margaux. He bought four hogsheads of Margaux at a time and one of Lafite every three months – at a premium of more than 20 per cent over ordinary claret. The value of his business to his wine merchant (whom he paid but rarely) was considerable.

The knowledgeable English wine merchant makes an early appearance on the scene. A classic claret buyer was "the most successful war profiteer of his age", James Brydges, the first Duke of Chandos, "the builder of the almost legendary" house of Canon, and "the patron of Handel". He "had a healthy curiosity in liquors" according to his biographers, and was obviously a very sophisticated drinker. He kept champagne, and at least two burgundies (*Nuits* and *vin de bon*); he hoped that one shipment of "O'Brian" "will improve in the keeping"; he used words like "body", "rich" and "thick and ropy" to describe the contents of his cellar. Most significantly he spotted a basic flaw which was to debase the "claret" sold to the English market for over a century: the way it was prepared, with the addition of stronger wines from the Rhône, from Spain, or perhaps Cahors, during and after fermentation, generally in the cellars below the Quai des Chartrons in Bordeaux. In the 1780s Thomas Jefferson assured a friend that the "Château

Margau of the year 1784" may have been expensive at 3 livres a bottle – but was "bought by myself on this spot and therefore genuine".

MARGAUX AS A MAJOR AGRICULTURAL BUSINESS

In 1694 François Delphin d'Aulède de Lestonnac, Baron de Margaux, who was known as the Marquis d'Aulède, succeeded his father. Like Ségur, d'Aulède owned several properties in Paris and Bordeaux, but the jewel in his crown was the estate of Margaux – which represented nearly half his total landed property. Moreover, thanks to the lucky survival of a crucial document, we know that he properly appreciated the château's wine. In the early 1700s, the then estate manager (*régisseur*) wrote down, probably for his own benefit, a lengthy memorandum significantly entitled "Memorandum on how to make Margaux's wines following Berlon's example".

Berlon, the *régisseur* at Margaux in the late seventeenth century, was one of the unsung heroes of the Médoc, and M. Pijassou was not exaggerating when he called him "the Dom Pérignon" of claret. Berlon's ideas, as faithfully transcribed by his successor, point up the changes he introduced, and the similarities – and vast differences – between the idea of "Margaux" then and now.

We know about the wine destined for the owner, "*le vin de provision*", because it was made quite separately from "*le grand vin*", "*le second vin*" and the wine made from grapes brought in by sharecroppers (*métayers*) as part of the seigneur's feudal rights. The Marquis kept for himself two *tonneaux* of wine – over a couple of thousand bottles – all made purely from grapes from the Puch Sem Peyre and the Cap de Haut. d'Aulède's wine was made purely from black grapes – itself unusual as even the *grand vin* still had a proportion, about a tenth, of white grapes in it, thus maintaining the old tradition that *clairet* was indeed lighter in colour than other red wines. But even the Marquis's wine was not really red: "a little deeper than rosé", according to Berlon's anonymous successor. The first step towards making a clear, fine, light claret for the Marquis was to ensure that all the stalks and woody matter were removed: again the method differed from

crucial factors in making modern claret: the age of the vines and the choice of specific varieties of wines with which to match the soil and location of different parcels of land. The history of Margaux relates that it was M. Joseph de Fumel, at the end of the eighteenth century, "who had noble varieties of vine planted in the vineyard".

Where Berlon was a distinct, and crucial, innovator was not merely in harvesting the white and black grapes separately, but also in making the wine from them in quite separate vats. One idea that was obviously crucial, then as now, was *terroir*, the exact spot where the grapes had grown. He carefully selected loads of grapes from the better parts of the *vignoble* and used them as the *pied de cuve*, the foundation for every vat, to increase the average quality of the wine. Another of Berlon's innovations was to ensure that both the juice and the *vendange*, the skins and stalks from the same load, were put in the same vat. In all these precautions we see – nearly three centuries ago – a recognition that the making of good wine depends as much on scrupulous care as on scientific progress.

Berlon's careful nursing of his wine continued with the *égalisage* – ensuring that the wine from different vats eventually sold by the estate was of a regular quality, as the all-powerful merchants wanted: "the merchants require that all the red wine should be the same". As usual, this involved the acquisition of special containers, enabling an exact mixture to be made from vats and casks of very different sizes, containers which themselves had to be properly bound to prevent oxidization. This in turn involved frequent topping up, often with the best of wines brought in from the estate's tenants. In all they paid 12 *barriques* of wine in feudal dues – of which the best two came from the estate of M. Lascombes, now a second growth, although the other wines were from less distinguished vineyards. Nevertheless, by using these wines where otherwise it would have wasted some of its better wine, the owner was profiting very considerably by upgrading the value of the rents paid by the tenants. The tenants paid only a fifth of their crop: the unfortunate *métayers* – sharecroppers – paid a half. Their wine was less distinguished – and they were considered lucky to get back the pressings with which they could

that used for any of the estate's other wines. The containers of grapes destined for *le grand vin* had some of their woody matter removed; grapes for *le second vin* were left largely untouched – clearly Berlon and his successors did not mind if the presence of a greater proportion of woody matter made *le second vin* more tannic and astringent than either of the two choicer wines. (Crucially, Berlon and his successors examined every hod of grapes closely to judge their quality). Finally, the Marquis's wine was only lightly fermented, for just 24 hours, before being moved to smaller casks.

Throughout the memorandum runs a strange mixture of practices which are still current today, others which are now unheard-of, and some of Berlon's own innovations. Of these the most important was the separation of red from white grapes. But even Berlon does not mention two

These two extremely rare bottles from 1771 and 1791 were opened in May 1987 in Los Angeles at a tasting of 70 vintages from Château Margaux.

then make their own *piquette,* the thin, unappetizing wine which has been the usual beverage of the working classes in the Médoc until recently.

By the 1740s a major Médocain estate was big business – almost entirely because of the value of the wine it produced. This is one of the many facts to emerge from one of the most fascinating sets of documents bequeathed to the wine historian by the French administrative machine. These concern the prolonged battle between François d'Aulède's second wife and the taxmen. After her husband's death she complained bitterly about the 1740s. In a good year, as the taxman pointed out, the profits were enormous: "Having sold the first and second wines for a total of 70,000 livres, to which should be added around 4,000 for the money coming in from feudal dues, and the leases of pastures and buildings, adds up to a total income of 74,000 livres; deducting about 12,000 in expenses leaves a net income of 62,000, on which only 5,000 livres is to be paid". Since the basic tax was the *dixième,* a tax of a tenth, the taxmen had some basis for feeling that the estate was being undertaxed. In a good year, the taxmen pointed

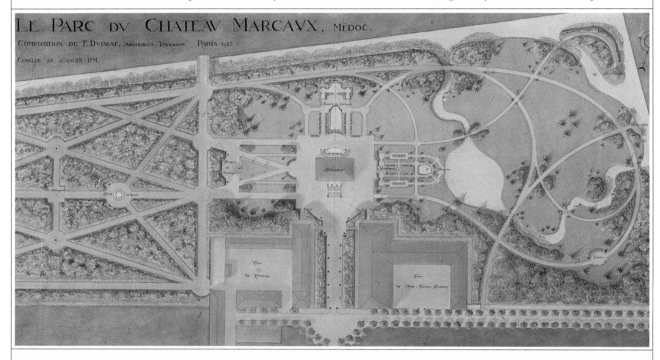

the allegedly excessive taxes paid by her husband in the first half of the 1740s and fought ferociously against the claim of over 20,000 livres made for back taxes – especially against a possible seizure of wine to pay the debt. What emerged from the subsequent correspondence was the colossal gap between good years and bad in the Médoc.

The Bordelais are often accused of having a "boom and bust" mentality, and one can see the historical origins of this outlook in the history of out, the expenses could be covered by rents and feudal dues, and the money – around 5,000 livres – from the sale of the *second vin,* leaving the proceeds from *le grand vin* as pure profit.

There was no denying, on either side, that the income from the wine was the decisive factor – even though the rest of the estate was considerable by any standards, the income was only 4,000 livres, a mere fifteenth of the enormous income brought in by the wine in a good one. But not

A plan for the gardens of Château Margaux à la française put forward by landscape architect M. F. Duprat in 1927 but only partially carried out.

Plan of part of the estate in 1759. The garden was first created by Olive de Lestonnac in the first half of the seventeenth century.

every year, as Madame d'Aulède insisted at length, was a good one. Her basic point was that the tax had been reckoned on a good year, but to listen to her you would believe that such miracles did not occur very often in a Médoc where either there was, seemingly, not enough wine to make a living, or too much, in which case the wine could not be sold but had to be kept at considerable expense for years on end.

Inevitably she made great play of her husband's great age, when the authorities wondered why she was arguing about taxes dating back half a decade or more. She reckoned that the total profit for the three years 1742-44 were a mere 19,000 livres. Yet on this 19,000, the late Marquis had had to pay 5,000 a year. He had not complained: "he never asked for a reduction because he had been ill" ever since the tax was increased from a twentieth to a tenth of revenues, on the outbreak of war; besides, he had hoped that the war would soon end, and the tax be reduced. As far as the two years immediately after his death were concerned, his widow claimed that these were so bad that "one produced scarcely enough to pay for the costs of the estate, and in the other the sale of the *grands vins* was pure loss". And, to add insult to injury, the impossible M. de Tourny had imposed a new tax on the Médoc to build a new road, a tax from which the seigneurs had previously been exempt.

In the event, the redoubtable widow got a substantial reduction – from 5,000 livres to 2,900 (for 1746 at least) but not before the tax authorities had ripped her case apart. In one instance they were able to use information from the merchants to show that she had sold the immense 1749 vintage at very high prices, for a sum which greatly exceeded her expenses, even though she had claimed it as one of the estate's many bad years. The merchants may have helped the tax authorities only indirectly, but their influence was certainly increasing. By the 1780s, one of them, Jernon, was powerful enough to take on a lease of Margaux for ten years, a commitment which depended on the possession of both capital and access to the English market.

To the social or economic historian, the exchanges show the power of the central government even when confronted by a redoubtable widow of some social clout – and thus the very limited freedom of even the most powerfully placed aristocrats. To the historian of Margaux, they are fascinating because they show how little things have changed: how the locals will always exaggerate their woes and tend to gloss over the good years (like 1749 – or 1970, or 1982) when a very large harvest is sold at a handsome price; how involved the owner was with the estate, even when he or she spent most of his or her time in Paris. And how, above all, the taxman is considered by the growers as merely another hostile element, like hail or rot, or late frosts.

THE DU BARRY CONNECTION

François d'Aulède died childless and at a great age. As a result the Margaux estate again passed through the female line. The heir was Louis, the eldest son of his sister Catherine, a distinguished soldier, *mousquetaire gris,* who was wounded at Malplaquet in 1711 (his brother Delphin had been killed the previous year at Oudernarde). Ironically, while the heirs-presumptive to the estate were fighting the English, the value of their future inheritance was increasing by leaps and bounds because of the enemy's thirst for its wine.

Louis de Fumel only inherited the estate a couple of years before his death in 1749 – and judging by his aunt's correspondence he did not have much say in running it – he died at Haut-Brion, not Margaux. But matters were different for his heir, Joseph de Fumel. Like his father, Joseph was a distinguished soldier. He became the King's lieutenant-general in Burgundy and by the 1770s he was back in Bordeaux as governor of the Château Trompette, the impressive fortress which was the symbol of the king's power in the city. Moreover, he was known to be immensely wealthy – and he had only one child, a daughter, Marie-Louise-Elizabeth.

The fame of Margaux – and the combined fortunes of the d'Aulède and Fumel families to which she was heir – served her badly, and ensured her unwilling participation in French history. For by the time she was of marriageable age, Louis XV was sick and old. His last mistress, Madame du Barry, knew perfectly well that no mercy would be shown her once her royal lover

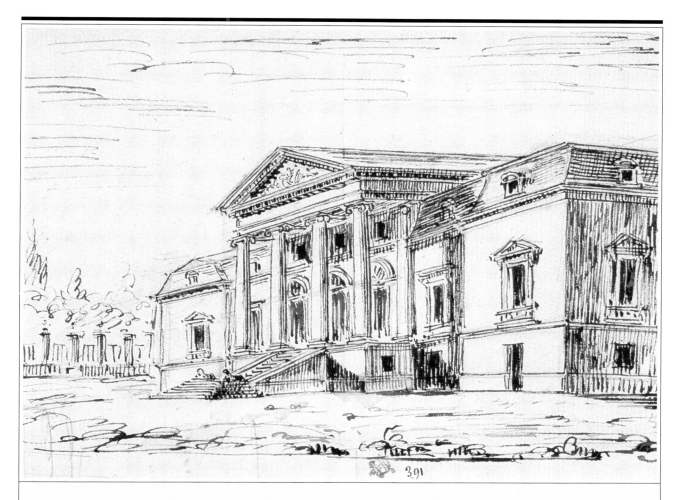

died. And inevitably the whole du Barry family felt the need to consolidate its fortunes while the King was still alive. The youngest of her brothers, Jean-Baptiste-Guillaume-Nicolas (usually called Elie) was much less of a wastrel than his two elder brothers and had trained to be an army officer. But his battle to win his heiress and to abandon a name which was sure to become a major impediment in the near future met severe problems. Namely, despite an honourable career, a financially secured future and, in addition, having been granted by his future father-in-law the reversion of the Governorship of Château Trompette, the young lady rejected the idea of marriage. At this point, in the words of a contemporary anecdotist: "the King was obliged to become involved, and the marriage duly took place; but the Fumel family still refused to let Dubarri take their name".

But not for long. Within three months of the death of his sister-in-law's royal protector Dubarri felt obliged to assume protective plumage (she herself had been imprisoned). Unable to use his father-in-law's name, he borrowed his mother-in-law's maiden names. She had been born Mademoiselle de Conty, and her father had been the Seigneur of Hargicourt in Flanders. So the Chevalier du Barri became – and remained – M. le Comte d'Hargicourt. As such he took his

One of Louis Combes' first plans for the main façade. This design was rejected on the basis that the peristyle, with its massive Ionic columns, was far too heavy for the building. M. Robert Coustet, the eminent architectural historian, suspects that in this sketch, Combes merely stuck a new façade on the existing château.

Château-Margaux (Margaux).

Château Margaux reflects perfectly the theories that Combes developed during his trip to Italy concerning classical buildings and the way in which they should be integrated into the landscape. In the words of the late Professor Pariset, Combes learned "how to blend the landscape and architecture, with its formal beauties and its long straight lines".

position with the greatest seriousness and obviously played an active role in the reassertion of feudal privileges which marked the last few years of the *Ancien Régime*.

THE REVOLUTION OF MARGAUX

For sheer human drama the story of Château Margaux during the 20 years after 1789 would be hard to surpass. At its most basic level, the Revolution marked the end of three centuries during which the property had never changed hands for money, but merely been passed down through a succession of families which were, at the very least, closely connected by marriage. As elsewhere in the world of Bordeaux wine, it also marked the virtual extinction of the influence of the families of *Parlementaires* who had dominated its major estates.

Not unnaturally, the first dramas connected with Margaux were human ones. The feudally-minded Comte d'Hargicourt was an early emigré. Legend has it that he returned, but his departure ended his association with Margaux – and as soon as he had emigrated, the property was sequestrated. His wife and father-in-law, more rooted to their homes, suffered more acutely. Joseph de Fumel had always been a paternalist and his generosity to the district earned him popularity. In 1791, he was proclaimed Mayor of Bordeaux by acclamation, but the burden of office proved so arduous in revolutionary times that he was forced to resign and retire to the Château of Haut-Brion, where he lived in the greatest simplicity and modesty, surrounded only by a few members of his family – the others, seven in number, having already emigrated. He was dragged from his retreat in November 1793 to be taken, with his family, to prison in Bordeaux, and from there to the Revolutionary scaffold where he was executed. His daughter also "died, a victim of the Law of Suspects, on the 6th February 1794, at the age of 44".

But that was not the end of the family: only two years later, the estate was bought back by Joseph de Fumel's formidable young niece, Laure Fumel. The estate she was taking back was in a miserable condition. For several years it had been let by the state to one Mathieu Miqueau, who seems

to have been even more ruthless than most of the *fermiers* (lessees) who took advantage of cheap leases of valuable sequestrated property to make their fortunes. Using the standard formula, which multiplied the actual or notional revenue from land by 18 or 22 times depending on the type of holding, the estate was valued at just over a million livres. Miqueau's depredations, neglect and the uncertain outlook had reduced its value by only 150,000 livres, less than 15 per cent of its pre-Revolutionary value.

Her first husband was himself to become famous. Count Hector Brane, known after the Restoration of 1815 as the "Napoleon of the Médoc", was owner at one time of the estate of Brane-Mouton in Pauillac, now known as Mouton-Rothschild, which he relinquished because he thought that another property, that of Brane-Cantenac, named after him in the commune of Cantenac, a couple of miles south of Margaux,

Beltran Douat, Marquis de la Colonilla.

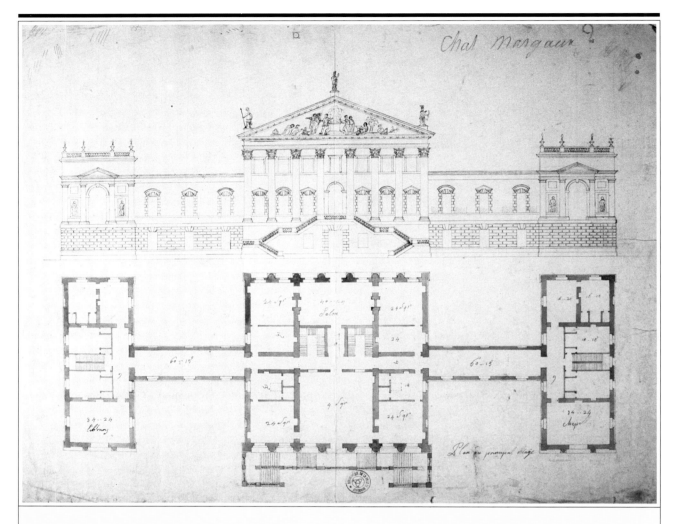

had better prospects. The problems he brought into Laure Fumel's life did not, however, emerge for some years. It was the government which created the immediate trouble. When she bought Margaux, Citoyenne Fumel could, in theory, pay in rapidly depreciating paper money, but her tenure was to be short. Within three months of recapturing her inheritance she had been forced to let it to pay an unexpected charge. Too many people had made too great a profit out of buying confiscated estates with paper money. So buyers were now to be forced to pay one quarter of the purchase price in metallic currency. She had to turn to the only group in Bordeaux which could help: the merchants on the Quais des Chartrons.

Three of the best-known, Henry Martin, Daniel Guestier, and the Macarthy brothers had in fact taken on the lease following Miqueau's disastrous tenure. The newly-weds had declared that they wanted to exercise their right to repossess – together with the minimal obligations attached to it. But at that point, the government stepped in with its new requirements, and the Branes had to fall back on a strengthened form of the same

Combes had plenty of room to experiment with the lay-out of the ground floor of the château. The idea of adding wings probably stems from an earlier commission to enlarge Château Olivier.

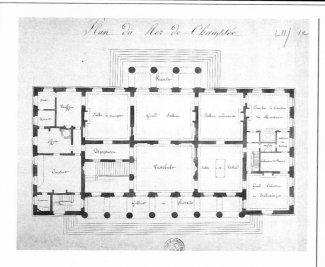

group. Henry Martin and Daniel Guestier were joined by Robert Forster and the partnership of Guestier – a relative newcomer – and the Johnston family. The 15 year lease was to last until 1811. In the lease agreement made, one clause was to lead to considerable trouble later: the lessees agreed to pay the taxes to which the estate had been liable in 1790. The lease was obviously very profitable; in a letter the next year, Barton, who had taken over Johnston's interests, writes that their return that year would be worth 34,000 livres (of which he was entitled to a half). Given that there were, effectively, two other partners, the profit for the year must have been around 100,000 livres.

Within two years the wretched Hector Brane, stripped of all his possessions, had to leave his wife and flee to Hamburg, though not before a son was born, on 12th October 1796, 18 months after the marriage. However, the estate of Château Margaux was not touched – it had been bought by Citoyenne Fumel, who had paid for it with her own money, on her own recognizances. Because she had bought the château before her marriage, it could not be treated by the government as part of her husband's estate. But because she had subsequently married Brane, the estate became their joint property and thus part of the assets which his creditors could claim if the time came.

Matters soon got much more complicated. As the wretched Brane wrote: "But as if my misfortunes were never going to end, I learnt while I was abroad of the divorce of Citoyenne Fumel and her proposed remarriage". Citoyenne Fumel had indeed chosen her next husband. He was a merchant called Langsdorff, whom she married on 9th November 1801. Remarriage naturally induced a desire to be rid of all the evidence of a past life. So she offered the lessees the chance to buy up the estate. They turned the offer down, wary of the long-term responsibilities – as did they and their brethren on a number of other occasions during the Revolutionary period. But Laure Langsdorff, as she had become after her second marriage, was in a hurry to sell. And within three months the estate had been sold at auction to a complete outsider, Bertran (or Beltran) Douat, Marquis de la Colonilla, supposed at the time to be a Spanish nobleman. He got it at a bargain price – 650,000 francs, not much more than half its pre-Revolutionary value, and 40 per cent less than the price Laure Fumel had had to pay. The sale was obviously extremely quick. Colonilla, who was then in Paris, had appointed a Bordeaux merchant, Jacques Gramont, as his agent, only on 17th February, ten days before the sale.

By then, however, the legalities surrounding the estate, what with the rights of the lessees, the debts accumulated over 20 years by Hector Brane, and the rights to the estate he had acquired through marriage to Mlle. Fumel, not to mention the law regarding the sale of *Biens Nationaux,* were so entangled that it took six and a half years

Further plans for the ground floor (left). The design for the ceiling of the peristyle (right) is one of the few areas where Combes allowed himself any form of decoration – even so, the decoration would have been invisible until the steps had been mounted.

for Colonilla finally to consummate the deal.

COLONILLA – AND THE ESTATE HE BOUGHT

There could, in theory, be no greater break with the past than that represented by the arrival at Margaux of Bertran Douat, Marquis de la Colonilla – at first sight a Spanish nobleman was taking over from the *haute bourgeoisie* of Bordeaux. In fact, the change was not as radical as it appears. Douat is a typical name in south-west France and peasants of that name feature on the historical maps of Margaux as landowners of scattered rows of vines. But for all his similarities to many previous château owners, he did not belong to either of the classes which had hitherto monopolized the Médoc: the *Parlementaires* (and their ten-

tacular families) and the merchants. In buying Margaux, Douat – the outsider – was setting a precedent which was to be widely followed. Beltran (to give him his proper name) Douat was in fact a Basque from Ciboure – near St-Jean-de-Luz, close to the Spanish frontier. In 1763, when he was 21, Beltran went to Bilbao, then a port much frequented by French ships, and after two years of travelling through Spain and Europe, settled there at the end of the 1760s with his younger brother.

The Douats prospered, as the local correspondents of the St-Charles's Bank, and as founders of a Maritime Insurance Company. In 1789, after a long battle, Beltran finally managed to buy his title. The sellers – the family of the Marquis de la Cruz, who had inherited a spare Marquisate – were only too willing to sell (since the title brought with it the need to pay additional taxes, and the family's financial problems had led it to seek help from the Douats anyway). There were plenty of local dignitaries prepared to assert that Beltran was fully worthy of the title. But again there was local opposition. Eventually the Marquis of Santa Cruz himself was made King's High Steward and the transfer went through. The title had been the Marquisate of Bayonne, but was changed to de la Colonilla – of the Colonies.

That was in 1789: and obviously a wealthy citizen living so close to the French frontier became involved in politics. Through his elder brother, who lived in Bordeaux, he received and helped a steady stream of refugees, many of them clerics. But he was too open-minded a man to be safe from anti-Revolutionary hysteria (among the supposedly subversive literature later found in his house was John Adam's *Defence of the American Constitution*. Moreover, he was a close personal friend of De Bourgoing, who was appointed French Ambassador to Spain at the beginning of 1792, and who, in his frequent letters to Douat, expressed himself very freely. It was not surprising, therefore, that the locals suspected him of Jacobin tendencies.

In September 1792, he was duly arrested on the orders of the central government – and the warrant also specifically required that his correspondence be seized as well.

He was in prison for nearly three months, despite pleas from his wife and doctors that the

Louis Combes, architect of Château Margaux.

Inevitably not all of Combes' designs were executed. Projects for a dovecot (opposite right) and a mock medieval entrance (opposite left) failed. The section of the château (bottom left) is the one that was finally executed.

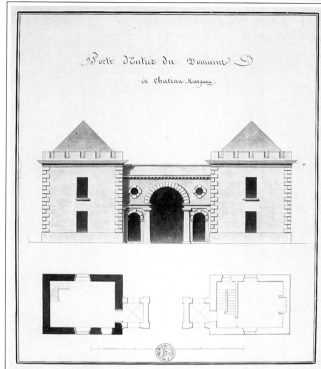

Porte d'Entrée du Domaine
de Château-Margaux

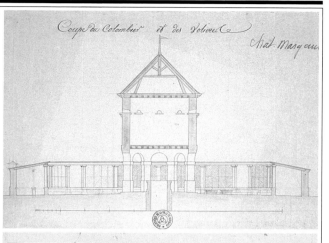

Coupe du Colombier et des Volières

Chat. Margaux

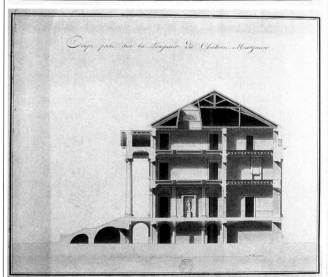

Coupe prise sur la Longueur du Château Margaux

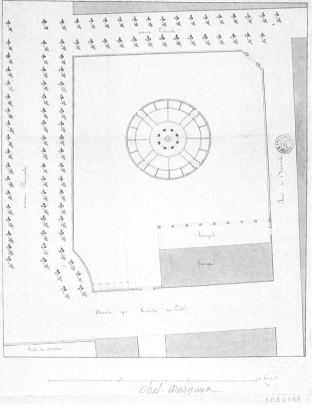

Chat. Margaux

"malignant fever" from which he suffered would lead to his death if he were not released – significantly, it took an intervention by Bourgoing to permit Douat to be sent home. Nevertheless, he was found guilty of revolutionary activities and was sentenced to four years' exile at a distance of at least 20 leagues (60 miles) from Bilbao, or any royal residence.

He retired unhurt to Burgos in the summer of 1793. Two years later he was pardoned – and the authorities virtually apologized for the sentence. Early in 1796 he was allowed to return home to Bilbao. By then he was in his late 50s, his wife had died, and he wanted, not unnaturally, to return to France. So he went to his brother in Bordeaux – although, judging from the addresses in Paris and Madrid from which he issued his instructions regarding the purchase of Margaux, he did not live there much. Indeed, the designs for his tomb are based on the assumption that he was to be buried in Paris.

Douat was interested more in the house and the estate than in its produce. And because of the inventories taken after the Revolution we know something about both at the time. The estate itself had not changed over the years. It was still over 500 acres; there was a sort of "home farm" (*domaine privé*) of over 150 acres, and it was clear, from the notional revenue figures, that the most productive land was in Margaux itself.

The house was completely different from the one built by Douat. There are no descriptions of it extant, but we can guess some idea of its size and shape from the inventory of the contents taken at the time of the sale. There were far fewer rooms on the first than on the ground floor – and there is no mention of more than one upper storey. A number of corridors are mentioned. At the end of one we find a *pavillon* or lodge and at the end of another a chapel, which must have been small because it contained only four chairs. So the house seems to have followed the pattern of a number of others in the Médoc, in being long and low, with the main reception rooms clustered towards the centre of the ground floor. This style is called a *chartreuse* by the locals.

As well as giving us some idea of the number and size of the rooms in the house, the inventory provides a fascinating glimpse into the relative values attached to different items of furniture at the time. The single most valuable item, "a fine bed with chintz covers" was worth 1,500 livres, nearly a tenth of the value of all the contents. There were three other beds each worth 800 livres, but none of these was in the master bedroom, where an alcove bed was worth 480 livres – the sort of price attached to a pair of horses or oxen.

Apart from beds, the only furniture worth much consisted of mirrors and a bookcase in *boiserie,* an item which today would be worth the most, but then was valued at only 1,200 francs. There were a number of fine mirrors, a chimney glass in one small salon, a valuable gold-framed, two-piece mirror in the *salon de printemps,* and another in the main drawing room. The dining room had a valuable mirror above the fireplace.

But there were only relatively few thinly scattered items for such a large house: obviously there had been losses since the Revolution. Apart from the 23 vats for making wine, and a full set of *douils, entonnoirs* and *bastes* (the local names for the containers, funnels and hods used in wine-making) the place seems to have been pretty bare. The kitchen used to feed the harvesters (the *cuisine de vendanges*), contained only a flour grinder. Equally the few beasts of burden mentioned in the inventory were obviously inadequate to serve as large an estate. But soon all this was to change. It did not take Colonilla long to decide that he wanted to build a new house on his estate. In March 1810, Giraud, his "factotum" in Bordeaux, wrote to the local architect Louis Combes. Giraud put himself forward as the person responsible for Combes' appointment and urged Combes to return quickly so that the work could begin as soon as possible; the Marquis was nearing 70, and was "an old man in a hurry". Within seven years Combes had created "a palace in the full sense of the word: a palace modelled on the Parthenon in Athens, with gracious Doric columns, magnificent carvings and a truly royal avenue". (Alfred Danflou, *Les Grand Crus Bordelais, 1867*).

A BANKABLE PROPOSITION

Beltran Douat died in September 1816, and it

leaving it to the merchants – who thus had control of the quality of the wine. Other châteaux, too, were able to profit far more from the great mid-century boom than was Margaux. Several times its owners, uninterested in the estate as a business, allowed its product to be *abonné* – sold under long-term contract (generally for ten years) at fixed prices – rather than playing a market which could be immensely profitable for the château.

Moreover, the owners did not, in general, think of Margaux as being of any great importance. For there was (and indeed there still is) a total contrast in scale and perspective in the importance of the châteaux of the Médoc as they are perceived from Bordeaux, and from Paris. To the Bordelais, the ownership of Château Margaux and its commercial policy mattered enormously. But to successive owners during the nineteenth and early twentieth centuries, Margaux was merely an investment to be visited at the appropriate time of the year to watch the *vendange,* but not central to the owner's business or social concerns. This is not to say that the owners were undistinguished; far from it. They were simply uninvolved.

The classic case of this paradoxical contrast is Alexandre Aguado, Marquis de las Marismas, the man who bought Margaux from Colonilla's three children in 1836. The price, 1,350,000 francs, was over double that paid by Colonilla. Nevertheless, it was only 150,000 francs more than the indestructible Hector Brane had obtained for Mouton – a second growth, lacking Margaux's majestic house and considerable estate – six years before. Alexandre Aguado, however, was no ordinary bargain-hunter; he was the first, and probably the most distinguished, of a long line of Parisian bankers – like the Rothschilds and the Pereires – who steadily bought their way into the Médoc in the middle of the nineteenth century.

Aguado, unlike Colonilla, was Spanish by birth. As a young army officer he had thrown in his lot with King Joseph and the Bonapartists. Naturally, after Napoleon's defeat, he was banished and fled to France. There, he made a colossal fortune as a banker: exploiting French influence in Spain in the 1820s, he arranged the whole of Spain's external debts, which were rationalized and quoted in every stock exchange in Europe under the name *Rentes Aguado* (Aguado Loans), making

seems highly unlikely that he had ever lived in the house he had built, for he died at his other property in the Bordelais, at Ambès. He left three children, about whom we know very little – except that the elder daughter married a noble French lawyer, Count Bastard d'Estang. But none seems to have had any great interest in the château – a reliable indication of a future in which the history of the château would be dominated by absentee, and largely uninvolved, landlords.

For a century after Colonilla's death, Margaux was not in the forefront of the history of the Médoc, as it had been a century earlier. It was left to Baron Brane to pioneer the introduction of the Cabernet Sauvignon grape which formed the basis for claret as we know it today. In the quarter-century after the Restoration of 1815 it was Lafite that consolidated its position as *premier des premiers* and it was other châteaux that introduced such innovations as bottling at the château, instead of

Alexandre Aguado, Marquis de las Marismas del Guadalquivir. He seems to have been less involved than other owners in the affairs of the estate – possibly because unlike others, it may not have been bought as a business proposition.

him an unpopular figure in Spain.

In the heyday of Ferdinand VII he gained the title of Marquis de las Marismas del Guadalquivir – "Marquis of the Marshes of the Guadalquivir": he was induced to finance the drainage of the marshes. But the title remained an empty one: a visit to Spain brought snubs from Spanish society and difficulties in carrying out his plans. Deciding that he was not receiving the consideration to which he considered himself entitled, he returned to Paris in a huff, gave up his role as Spain's international financial agent, and was naturalized as a French citizen in 1828. He kept up his banking activities but, for the rest of his short life (he was only 43 when he was naturalized, and died a mere 14 years later) he concentrated on the conspicuous – and exceedingly tasteful – consumption of the fortune he had earned.

His most famous possession was the Château of Petit-Bourg near Paris, which he restored: his lasting legacy to France was the bulk of his magnificent collection of Spanish and Italian pictures, which are now in the Louvre, in the appropriately named Aguado gallery. Among this collection of possessions and connections, Margaux seemingly did not shine brightly.

Naturally, the Aguados ensured that Margaux was properly decorated according to their taste – and since their ownership extended right through the reign of Napoleon III, the imprint was what we describe as "Second Empire". Indeed when the Ginestet family took over the house just before the World War II, it was still decorated in that taste. Their restoration efforts were naturally directed at ensuring some uniformity of style appropriate to the date of the original decoration, rather than that of the house's construction. A visitor in the 1860s remarked how the "state" apartments on the mezzanine floor were "furnished with an Asiatic ostentation, decorated with paintings by famous masters, like a museum, the entrance hall leading into these apartments was embellished with statues and panoplies. On the second floor were the master rooms, tastefully furnished, then the library which housed some fine books and a sixteenth-century pendulum clock". The style set in the middle of the nineteenth century prevailed until the Ginestets sold the estate in 1977, although the library was moved from the second floor down to the mezzanine in the course of the century.

The grandeur of the house, combined with the magnificence of the *chais,* indeed of the estate as a whole, made Margaux the showpiece of the Médoc in the nineteenth century. As late as 1934, after the motor car had made the whole of the Médoc far more accessible to visitors, the English wine-lover, Maurice Healy noted that because Margaux was the nearest of the estates to Bordeaux it was the first destination of many wine-lovers.

Comte Pillet-Will.

In fact it was the "staff" and not the proprietors who bore the brunt of the tourists. For Aguado himself lived mostly in Paris, as did his heirs, who were among the brightest ornaments of Parisian society. And it was a woman, his elder daughter-in-law, who dominated the scene until she sold the estate in 1879. Emily Macdonnell was a Scottish beauty who had married Aguado's eldest son, also called Alexandre. She became one of the most faithful of the six high-born, much envied, Ladies of the Palace attached to the Empress Eugénie, two of whom attended the Empress every week. According to a British journalist E. A. Vizetelly (writing under the pseudonym of *Le petit homme rouge*) Mme. Aguado was "a famous court beauty, with fair golden hair, a light dazzling complexion and a most graceful figure. But she was gradually borne down by successive misfortunes. First her husband, a naturalized Frenchman of Spanish origin and extremely wealthy, lost his reason, whereupon she would not suffer him to be removed to an asylum, but watched over him till his death. A new life seemed to be opening for her when, by special dispensations, she married her deceased husband's brother, Vicomte Onésime Aguado, but she lost in succession her lovely daughter, Carmen Duchess of Montmorency, then both her sons and her second husband also".

Madame Aguado loyally followed her mistress into exile to England after the Emperor was dethroned in 1870. Napoleon III died three years later; and any hopes of a Bonapartist Restoration were finally dashed when the Emperor's only son, the Prince Imperial, was killed fighting in the British army against the Zulus in 1879. That year Madame Aguado sold Château Margaux. Clearly she saw no reason to maintain any links with a country in which neither she nor her mistress would ever live again.

It cannot have been much of a consolation to her that in her hour of grief she struck a shrewd bargain. The possession of châteaux in the Médoc was still popular among the Parisian banking community. Moreoever, the local merchants, who had hesitated to buy even the most famous estates at bargain prices during the Revolutionary era, were themselves active buyers.

By that time, it had become clear that a major estate in the Médoc could be exceedingly prof-

itable – as indeed it had been before the Revolution. Obviously a considerable proportion of the profits went to the merchants, especially when they took on long-term contracts (*abonnements*). Margaux's wines had been *abonnés* for ten years before Aguado had bought the Château. In common with many of the others, they had also been *abonnés* for ten years from 1844 to 1853. But then came a double boost for the Médoc: the British stepped up their purchases of wine – the duty was sharply cut to 1 shilling per gallon in the early 1860s (2 pence per bottle) – and supplies dried up. For a few years, the oidium, a mushroom growth, devastated the vines: production of the *grand vin* at Margaux, which had averaged around 80 *tonneaux* in the ten years 1843-52, dropped to an average of 30 *tonneaux* during the five following years before the disease was mastered by a simple sulphur spray. But, as so often happens in the Médoc, any form of natural disaster led to such massive replanting that production soon outstripped the pre-disaster levels.

So it was with the oidium. The average production in the 1860s, at nearly 130 *tonneaux*, was 50 per cent greater than it had been before the oidium, and it rose another ten per cent in the two following decades. Moreoever, prices had risen substantially. Margaux had been *abonné* at a mere 2,100 francs per *tonneau* in the 1840s. In the good years of the 1850s and early 1860s, the wines were regularly fetching over double that price, and the levels reached during the years of shortage were held or even surpassed when production rose after oidium had been mastered.

Unfortunately for the Aguados, alone of the major proprietors in the Médoc, they granted a ten year *abonnement* from 1863 to 1872. This covered a decade which in the event proved to be the most profitable the Médoc would enjoy for a century. Margaux was *affermé* at a fixed price of 4,200 francs per *tonneau* (itself double the price obtained for much smaller vintages before the oidium struck). But other *crus* fetched prices of up to 6,000 francs, especially in the "super boom" year of 1868. Nevertheless, Margaux, like the other estates, could be exceptionally profitable: in 1865, and again in 1869, it produced over 175 *tonneaux* of *grand vin*. In a good year, the estate's total revenue, including that from the second wines, was over 400,000 francs. The majority of that sum was pure profit, since the costs of labour, casks and other major items were relatively stable – according to M. Pijassou's calculations not much more than a quarter of the revenue.

The returns, however, were not stable – as in the eighteenth century, a good year was often followed immediately by a dreadful one. The combination of a small harvest and lower prices reduced the return to the estate by two-thirds between 1872 and 1873. Nevertheless, in an age when money was all-important, the Médoc held obvious attractions for the capitalist classes, in Paris as well as Bordeaux.

The fact that the profits came from estates which bore famous names was obviously a bonus. Aguado's own purchase was made before the Médoc, in general, or Margaux in particular, had established a proper "track record" of profitability following the troubles of Revolutionary times, so the prestige element was probably more important for him than it was for later investors.

The Rothschilds had paid 4.4 million francs for Lafite in 1868, so a price of five million francs for Margaux was not, at first sight, unreasonable. The cost per hectare of vines, at 83,000 francs was, admittedly, over a third more than the Rothschilds had paid a decade earlier. But, at the time, the purchase seemed merely a confirmation of a trend which had been accelerating for half a century, not the landmark it proved to be in the economic history of the Médoc.

The buyer of Margaux, Comte Pillet-Will, was an almost copybook image of the average purchaser of a major Médocain estate in the last half of the nineteenth century. He was a Regent of the Banque de France, the innermost bastion of the French financial aristocracy. The family bank had been founded by his father, a native of Savoy, originally called simply Michael Pillet. He had added the name of the owner of the bank for which he worked in Lausanne before he moved to Paris in 1809. The Pillet-Wills were unlucky, for they bought Margaux at almost the precise moment when the tide of prosperity turned, resulting in an unprofitable ebb which lasted nearly 80 years.

In the 1870s and 1880s the Médoc was hit by three major blights: the great world slump, the mildew and phylloxera. The slump had started in 1873, well before the sale, and had already severely affected the market for claret. The owners would have been glad of the shelter afforded by an *abonnement;* even the marvellous 1875 vintage fetched only 3,500 francs a *tonneau;* the superb 1899 vintage fetched a mere 2,200 francs; the enormous and even better 1900 1,150 francs.

The situation was worsened by the mildew which ruined the first half-dozen in 1886 – by a simple copper sulphate spray, the *Bouillie Bordelaise.*

The most notorious of the three plagues of the Médoc was the phylloxera, a tiny louse which attacked the roots of the vines. Eventually, virtually every vine in France was replaced by plants grafted onto American stock which was immune from the pest. But this desperate, capital-intensive step was taken only very belatedly in the better estates of the Médoc. For the first 20 years after the pest's widespread appearance in the Médoc around 1880, the better growths fought to avoid replanting – which they feared would ruin the quality of the wine – by using every possible alternative.

These included injecting the roots of the vine and manuring far more heavily than had historically been considered desirable, so, precisely at the time that the bottom had dropped out of the market, yields soared. After completing a statistical analysis of yields at Margaux, a wine broker, William Lawton, estimated that Margaux's production had risen two and a half times in just over half a century. In fact he was being conservative, – the fabled 1893 vintage was the biggest ever, 400 *tonneaux,* nearly have a million bottles, and over five times the average production of the decade before the oidium arrived in the 1850s.

Of course 1893 was an exceptional year. Like 1970 (but remarkably few others) it combined superb quality with enormous quantity. But, even excluding 1893, the figures were astonishing. Whereas in the 1870s 80 hectares of vines had produced an average of 142 *tonneaux* of *grand vin* – something over 150,000 bottles – at the turn of the century the estate was producing an average of 225 *tonneaux* from 92 hectares: 60 per cent more wine from 15 per cent more vines. The yield of *grand vin* had leapt from 16 to 22 hectolitres per hectare – from under 870 to nearly 1,200 bottles for every acre of vines. And these figures did not include the 40 *tonneaux* of *seconds vins* produced by the estate. Nevertheless, despite the considerable increase in production, it was a mere half of the level now allowed by the French wine laws.

By the turn of the century the Pillet-Wills had become heavily dependent on Pierre Moreau, a broker, who from 1896 on had become increasingly responsible for buying the estate's wines – and he, in turn, had become more and more involved in Margaux rather than in other wines.

Margaux, like most of its fellows, was caught up in the wave of *abonnements* which swept Bordeaux in 1907 and lasted right through World War I. Although the prices were still pitifully low, these *abonnements* were at least a sign that trade was improving. This interest was artificially stimulated by the continuing effects of the phylloxera. The replanting, finally and reluctantly undertaken by the estates during the first two decades of the twentieth century (at Margaux up to ten acres a year were replanted), led to considerably reduced yields – at Margaux production halved within a few years – and the resultant relative shortage of wine obviously encouraged the growers. The replanting had another long-lasting effect on a handful of major estates including Margaux. The new young vines planted in such quantities could not produce grapes worthy of the estates' *grands vins* for at least ten years. But the wine they produced was perfectly palatable, and in the first decade of the century some of the wine formerly sold in wood as *second vin* was actively marketed in bottles – in Margaux's case as "Le Pavillon Rouge de Château Margaux". The second brand has not been marketed continuously since then, but has recurred whenever an especially conscientious owner has wanted to downgrade a sizeable percentage of his wine.

Unfortunately for the estate, the combination of a shortage of *grand vin* and, more especially the contract renewed at the nadir of France's war-time fortunes in 1917, prevented Margaux from taking advantage of the subsequent post-war boom which affected claret as it did almost every other commodity. All the efforts of the owners could not break the merchants' determination to adhere to the contracts they had negotiated a couple of years previously.

It was the Duc de la Tremoille, Pillet-Will's son-in-law, who took over as the member of the family responsible for Margaux on Pillet-Will's death in 1911. Tremoille was no ordinary duke; he was a left wing radical member of parliament for the Gironde. His interest in Margaux disappeared after he was defeated in the parliamentary elections of late 1919. Eighteen months later Tremoille sold out to a syndicate from the Herault.

THE LOCALS – AND THE STRUGGLES

The owners of Margaux in the nineteenth and twentieth centuries – the aristocratic bankers and capitalist consortia respectively – formed a total contrast. And whatever the estate has lost in aristocratic *éclat*, it has – spasmodically – gained in local involvement. The contrast was established immediately with the syndicate assembled by Pierre Moreau in the course of 1920 to buy the estate, which they did that year. The price was not unreasonable – a mere 4.5 million francs. Because the franc had depreciated so rapidly since 1914, this was far less than the 5.5 million paid by Frederick Pillet-Will 41 years previously. The estate had not changed greatly: it was described as being of 504 acres, plus another 70 acres consisting of the Ile d'Issan, historically part of the estate. According to the 1922 edition of Cocks and Feret's guide, a record 227 acres consisted of vines, an area which clearly included a great deal of land unworthy of the château's reputation.

The group formed a limited company, *La Société Viticole de Château Margaux,* with a nominal capital of 3 million francs. This was divided into 300 shares, each involving, nominally, an investment of 1,000 francs, although the shareholders subscribed only 2,250,000 francs. The leader of the syndicate was Albert Isenberg, a leading shipowner in Sète (he was the honorary Belgian Consul there), who started with over 170 shares. Pierre Moreau and his brother Roger do not seem to have had more than a fifth of the capital – and the remaining shares went to other local shipowners in Sète.

Nevertheless, the two dominant figures were clearly Isenberg and Pierre Moreau – helped by a remarkable *maître de chai*, Marcellus Grangerou, grandfather of the *maître de chai* in recent years,

Jean Grangerou. Moreau was in charge. Isenberg, for his part, arranged the financing of the loans required to bridge the gap between the sale price and the equity funds subscribed by the partners. The official Crédit Foncier put up 1,200,000 francs. But the remainder had to be borrowed for three years at the then exorbitant rate of interest of ten per cent. As one of the conditions of the loan, the partners had to insure the property against hail.

Moreau was obviously a man of ideas and innovations. The changes in the 1929 edition of Cocks and Feret speak volumes on the double objective of Moreau's plans. There is no mention of the total production of wine, nor of "Pavillion Rouge" (or "Blanc" for that matter). Spurred on by a pressing need for short-term profits, Moreau took the opportunity afforded by the maturation of the immediate post-phylloxera generation of vines to increase production very considerably and to use virtually all of the new production in the *grand vin*. The remaining quantities of *second vin* were sold in cask, not marketed as a separate brand.

The average quality of *grand vin* obviously suffered from this relaxation in the discipline so especially necessary at Margaux, yet this lapse could be repaired. Moreau's more positive initiatives had greater long-term significance. For the 1929 edition of Cocks and Feret proudly announced that the *grand vin* was "château bottled, with all the brands and seals of origin of the company which owns it". Thanks to the unlikely partnership of Moreau and the young Baron Philippe de Rothschild mandatory château bottling arrived in the Médoc during the 1920s, marking a revolutionary development in the relationships between the merchants and the growers.

As a broker Moreau was in a uniquely favoured position to see how far the châteaux were being exploited by the merchants. By selling their wines as soon as possible after fermentation – in fact, immediately after the brokers had confirmed its quality (*agréage*) – the growers were allowing the merchants the maximum freedom to "stretch" them while they matured and during the *assemblage* when the new wines are selected and blended before bottling. They had, historically, surrendered control over the quality of the product being sold to the public in the name of their property, and had also allowed the merchants to take the vast majority of the profits available from the wine. The proprietors' motives were obvious: they needed spot cash to pay their bills, and the additional capital required to keep the wine and nurse it through its first couple of years.

The only exceptions – the bankers who owned some of the better *crus* – were unprepared to invest more capital in properties which had been losing money for generations. The Rothschilds of Lafite, in particular, were unlikely to follow any return to mandatory château bottling after an earlier attempt in the 1880s which had resulted in the 1884 vintage turning sour in the bottles and being returned to the château en masse by the buyers.

The new Rothschild at Mouton was a different matter. In his own words, Baron Philippe wrote: "I was horrified to discover that I had no control over my product". Moreover, he owned an estate that had been classed as a second growth in 1855, and it had already become an obsession to rectify what he clearly saw as a major historical injustice. So he responded eagerly to Moreau's idea that the leading growths of the Médoc should simultaneously adopt château bottling, together with the challenge to the hitherto all-powerful merchants on the Quais des Chartrons represented by such a step. For him there was another crucial advantage: by acting as one of the two initiators of the idea of a *Groupement des Grands Crus* his wine would be automatically associated with Margaux, Lafite, Latour and Haut-Brion.

So it proved. Mouton, Margaux and Haut-Brion declared château bottling compulsory for their 1924 vintage, and Latour agreed to join from 1925. Only Lafite remained adamant: the château's "folk-memory" of the trauma with the 1884 vintage was still vivid. Moreau was given the task of winning round the Rothschild of Lafite and, in the spring of 1925, after a barrage of powerful and compelling arguments, they were persuaded to take up compulsory bottling at Lafite.

Pierre Moreau and Philippe de Rothschild trumpeted their success through the public announcement of the formation of what was effectively a new grouping. On 18th April 1925 nearly 100 leading lights in the world of wine, the buyers of the 1924 vintage, journalists and the all-important brokers, spent a day on a vinous pilgrimage.

The Ginestet family (top); Fernand Ginestet (left) one of Bordeaux's heroes; and (right) his son Pierre.

Their first stop was at Haut-Brion, to refute the rumours that the owner was selling the vineyard for development, then north to Margaux, where a lavish lunch was served. Thirsts were quenched by the jugs of "Pavillon Rouge" and "Blanc" on the tables. The opener was a 1906 Haut-Brion, followed by the 1899 Mouton-Rothschild, Latour of the same marvellous year, the exquisite 1900 Margaux in magnums, a dream parade of wines concluded by the legendary 1865 Lafite.

It was a truly historic occasion: a formal declaration of independence by the group of five *grands crus,* who "had sworn not to let out of their cellars any wine other than in bottles furnished with corks properly stamped with labels registered as trade marks and authentic capsules". In the afternoon, the party progressed royally round the three *grands crus* in Pauillac.

The five were joined a month later by Bertrand de Lur Saluces who owned Yquem, to become *L'Union des six grands crus classés de la Gironde – les six.* They hammered home their common sales policy with a series of additional clauses: the buyers were to contribute to the costs and the sellers retained the right not to sell their wine if they felt it was unworthy of its name – even if it fulfilled all the legal qualifications that it was fit for public consumption and was the genuine product of the château whose name it bore.

The Bordeaux trade was, predictably, furious. The lesson was rubbed in when the 1925 reception was repeated the next year – at Lafite – and again in the following year at the ultra-fashionable Pré Catalan restaurant in the Bois de Boulogne outside Paris. "*Le tout Paris*" attended – including ministers, members of the French academy, and a sizeable group of members of parliament, who were being lobbied by wine-growers to pass laws protecting France's better wines, regulations which finally reached the statute book in the 1930s. Before they did, it was almost impossible to pursue fraudulent merchants effectively.

But Moreau's initiative could not survive the harsh economic realities of the slump of the 1930s, the lack of continuity in the syndicate he had assembled, and, a final blow, an unprecedented series of three consecutive appalling vintages. Isenberg had died, and his shares had passed to a relative, uninterested in a venture

which was proving less and less profitable, so he sold most of his inheritance to a local grower, "Père" Recapet, owner of Brane-Cantenac. The late Marcel Grangerou remembered him as more interested in the blacksmith's forge and the other workshops in the *cour des artisans* than in the wine or its making. Although M. Recapet, and his son-in-law M. Lurton, finally owned nearly 40 per cent of the shares, neither they nor Moreau had enough capital to acquire the whole of the estate, let alone to re-establish the quality of its wine.

It was left to Fernand Ginestet, one of the most important and, indeed, heroic figures of Bordeaux in the twentieth century, to rescue the estate. Like Moreau, Ginestet was of humble local origin. But in a business still strongly influenced by aristocratic Anglo-Saxons he had succeeded by exploring new markets, in France itself and in its colonies. Moreover, rather than pursue the traditional policy of browbeating the growers, he had tried to

During his first visit to France in 1962, Chancellor Adenauer visited Château Margaux. He was given a magnum of Château Margaux 1876 – the year of his birth.

establish a common front between them and the trade with a series of initiatives – including the formation of the *Union des propriétés et du commerce,* the first joint organization bringing the two together in Bordeaux's history. With a number of other merchants, he had also founded a company, the *Société des Grands Crus Bordelais,* to buy up Médocain estates. But the company was badly run, and by the 1930s had been virtually liquidated, leaving Ginestet with a number of properties, but no ready cash.

His connection with the wealthy colonists in what was then French Indo-China however, provided him with the backing to acquire a majority shareholding in Margaux. Since 1815 the Bordeaux trade has never had enough ready cash to buy any of the first growths. Even at the height of the 1860s boom it took a group of merchants to find the funds which forced the Rothschilds to pay so much for Lafite. But his importer in Saigon, M. Boylandry, the Mayor of Saigon, not only had the requisite funds, but also trusted Ginestet implicitly.

In 1934, when Ginestet found that the estate was on the market, he despatched an immensely long telegram to Boylandry, explaining the proposition in detail, including an exact account of the tangled web of debts, loans and mortgages with which the estate had become festooned after five dreadful years for the growers. Boylandry was bewildered by the length and complexity of the proposition. He simply asked *Combien?*, agreed the sums involved, and telegraphed the money next day. Moreover, he left Ginestet and his son Pierre in control, although they owned only a minority of the shares.

Pierre Ginestet.

The Ginestets set to work with a will. Because their tenure of the estate ended so unhappily 40 years later, it is easy to forget the improvements they effected in the estate, in its wines, and in the house itself, during the first 20 years of their control. The most dramatic change was in the shape of the property as shown by the figures in Cocks and Feret: the 227 acres of vines in the 1928 edition reduced to 148 in 1949 (although the estate remained the same size). Ginestet took advantage of the depressed levels to which land prices had naturally fallen (and, in particular, of the financial problems of the Delor family which owned Durfort-Vivens) to reconstruct the estate. He bought back valuable acreage in a series of exchanges, especially with Rausan-Ségla. He brought into the estate some of the holdings of Château Abel Laurent, which lay between the Château and Palmer. In all he reduced the estate to the compact package of first-class *terroir* it had been before the sprawl started in the late nineteenth century.

The changes in the *grand vin* were even more marked. When they arrived, the Ginestets found that the 18 fermentation vats each had a copper pipe leading to a single outlet. The wine impartially obtained from each vat flowed through a single copper tap to the casks in which it was to mature. This arrangement made nonsense of the tradition, established in Berlon's time nearly two and a half centuries earlier, that the *grand vin* was assembled from a careful selection of wines. Ginestet promptly dismantled this apparatus and reversed the desperate policy of maximum production of *grand vin* by which Moreau had tried to combat the economic effects of the slump.

He did not, however, restore the idea of "Pavillon Rouge" (although he maintained the "Pavillon Blanc"). He was wily enough to use the *second vin* in the blend bearing the name of the commune rather than the château sold by his firm – the "Margaux" of F. Ginestet. Buyers were therefore encouraged to buy the branded wine by the – quite legitimate – thought that it contained a proportion of wine from the vines of the château itself.

When the Ginestets took over, the workers had not been paid for six months, and Lawton's records show the painful slowness of sales and the low prices to which the slump had reduced even the finest wines. Fortunately, they were able to rely, for running the estate, on the inherited skills of the Grangerou family. Marcellus's son, Marcel, took over as *maître de chai* just before the war, and his son, Jean, is still in the same job.

It took the Ginestets nearly 20 years to restructure the estate and restore the 1855 boundaries: by then, Boylandry had died, and his estate was divided between a second wife and a son born to him by an earlier Chinese spouse. The Ginestets were able to persuade them to sell: and even M. Lurton, M. Recapet's son-in-law, who had received no dividend or profit more than 20 years after his father-in-law had made his first investment in the estate, was prepared to give up – a piece of bad timing which leaves his son, Lucien Lurton, the owner of Brane-Cantenac, sad and pensive to this day. The Lurtons exchanged their shares in Margaux, still nearly 40 per cent of the total, for Clos Fourtet, itself one of the finest estates in St-Emilion.

Only a couple of years after buying the remaining shares in the estate, the Ginestets were finally able to return to the practice of compulsory bottling at the château. Even in the first post-war years, some of the *grand vin* (and a good deal of the wine from the family's other properties, notably Cos d'Estournel) had been exported in cask to a few select importers whom the family could trust, in Belgium and in countries where it was either impossible to import wine in bottles or where the duties were prohibitive. But as late as 1950, a scandal broke out in Belgium and the family then decided on compulsory bottling at the château from, and including, that year's vintage.

After the estate and the wine came the château. It was not until after the war that the family moved into the house, and they spent a great deal of time and effort in restoring the house and gardens to the pristine splendour they had enjoyed under the Aguados. For the idea that the château was the "Versailles of the Médoc" remained, and this ensured that it was the natural venue for any major celebration involving Bordeaux.

But the very originality of the Ginestets, the refusal to conform with Bordeaux's accepted ideas from Fernand Ginestet inherited by Pierre and his son Bernard, together with the family's scrupulous sense of honour, proved their undoing in the end. In the 1960s, when the traditional elements in the trade formed a loose cartel (Group A), to monopolize the marketing of the major estates they owned, only the Ginestets really played the game. Then Pierre broke the rules – he proposed to blend the problematic 1965 *grand vin* with some of the much tougher (*corsé* – full-blooded) wine produced in 1964 and 1966, and sell it as Château Margaux without a date.

Outsiders condemned this initiative as breaking one of the fundamentals in the production of great wine. Pierre Ginestet puts the blame on the other members of Group A: they preferred, he asserts, to sell vintages rather than châteaux. They were jealous and worried because they made their living by spotting the potential quality of good years earlier than outsiders and then speculating on them: "they were selling numbers rather than wine" is how he sums it up. Despite a major marketing effort, the initiative blotted the Ginestets' copybook in the eyes of many in the wine trade outside the charmed circle of Group A.

During the 1960s, too, the discipline so necessary to the maintenance of a major estate slackened as the then *régisseur,* M. Delhomme, aged. There was little or no re-planting, so yields from the best parts of the estate – notably the Cap de Haut – diminished, and the proportion of wines from other parts of the estate consequently increased. Things started to get better with the appointment of Jean-Pierre Blanchard as *chef de culture;* in the early 1970s, he started a major programme of planting. This involved over 35,000 new vines in seven years, but was mostly confined to replacing vines that had died or were dying – whole plots were not dug up.

At the end of the 1960s Pierre's second son, Bernard, wrote a powerful paper in which he analysed with surgical precision the reliance of Bordeaux's wine trade on out-of-date sales methods and cumbersome marketing chains, and condemned his fellows for refusing to come to terms with the modern world. For himself, he advertised the firm's wines, and personalized them as *signé Ginestet* in a series of advertisements which shocked other merchants to the core.

Unfortunately, in the logical pursuit of his ideas, Bernard committed the family firm to competing with the numerous international groups which had invaded Bordeaux in the course of the 1960s, and whose presence had prevented Group A from making its control effective. As demand – and prices – leapt upwards in the first years of the 1970s, the merchants were forced back on a more sophisticated version of the old *abonnement* system to guarantee supplies of wine from individual estates. But the tables had turned completely: the growers could afford to choose between the lucrative contracts with which they were being wooed, and the – potentially even more profitable – sale of their wines on an annual basis. By contrast the merchants, whether native or outsiders, were desperate for regular supplies of wine which they could market as brand names. And Ginestet was the only firm to compete in the big time with Seagrams, Allied Breweries, International Distillers & Vintners and Bass Charrington, groups which loomed large even in international terms, and were unprecedently rich by Bordeaux standards.

Even worse, there were family problems. At the end of the 1960s, the family's properties had been divided. Pierre Ginestet's sister, Madame Prats, had taken as her share all the family's other estates, headed by Cos d'Estournel, leaving Pierre and Bernard with Margaux. But Pierre, who was as old as the century, had tried to minimize fiscal problems by leaving the estate to his eldest son, whose mental state led him to take his own life in 1972. So the family was faced with succession duties combined with the need to find increasing amounts of capital. The boom of the early 1970s overheated, and in 1973 came the crash. For over two years the Ginestets struggled to find the funds with which to buy the enormously large 1973 and 1974 vintages from the châteaux whose entire production they had contracted to purchase, but which was literally unsaleable anywhere in the world. The Ginestets were the only major holder of contracts not backed by major outside capital resources: and they were among the few who behaved like gentlemen in honouring every one of their contracts. But by 1975 the situation was clearly hopeless. The family had been forced to borrow over 50 million francs – an amount greater than their firm's annual turnover – in order to honour their obligations. They were forced to look for a buyer for their most precious possession – indeed the only one worth anything at all in those distressful days – Château Margaux.

Double page following: Under the ownership of André Mentzelopoulos the château, the estate and the wine has been transformed in a way that it has never previously enjoyed in its long history.

THE
RENAISSANCE OF
MARGAUX

THE GINESTETS' TRIUMPHANT GAMBLE

Critics of the Bordeaux wine trade have always accused it of consisting too largely of gamblers, poker-players nursing their relatively slender capital resources until they had the chance to stake their all on a promising vintage. The accusation has a lot of weight behind it, but sometimes nerve and the willingness to hang on and hope against hope are essential. And never were these attributes displayed tobetter advantage than by Pierre and Bernard Ginestet during the two agonizing years it took them to sell their precious estate.

They were fighting against the market — weighed down with wines from the two enormous vintage of 1973 and 1974. Because sales of fine wine, except at distress prices, virtually ceased for a couple of years, the Ginestets had almost no cash flowing in to balance the interest on their debts – 20,000 francs every day. They were fighting the French political, economic and commercial establishment, which seemed oblivious to their feelings, or even their desire not to be driven out of business. The Ginestets' strategy was simple: they accepted the need to sell the estate, but they wanted to retain their business and to ensure that any buyer would not disturb the family's 40-year monopoly of sales of the château's wines. Moreover, it was natural that the septuagenarian Pierre would want to end his days in serenity, in the château he had done so much to restore. If the worst happened, and they had to part with the family wine business as well, then they would at least want a guarantee of continuity of employment for their workers. During two long years no organization owned or controlled by Frenchmen or the French state came near to fulfilling their minimum conditions.

By the end of 1975 they were in touch with Clifford Bell, the managing director of the American liquor business, National Distillers, and by April they had concluded a deal with his company. The Americans were prepared to meet all the family's conditions. At that point the French government turned really nasty. The official position spelled out in August 1976, when permission was officially refused, was that the takeover would endanger the position of the whole French wine trade, and that the American firm "would not fail to use the brand name of Château Margaux to promote no matter what type of merchandise". Nevertheless, according to the Ginestets, the Ministry of Finance assured them that they would not suffer from the ban, but that an equivalent offer from French sources could be found.

Within the next few weeks, it became painfully apparent that these were empty assurances and the government handed the problem to the Crédit Agricole, the state-owned agricultural bank which was one of the family's major creditors. The bank suggested a price of 60 million francs – for both estate and business – which would only have covered the family's debts, and provided none of the assurances they sought. The Ginestets decided on a final effort: to put the estate up for auction. Christie's and Knight, Frank & Rutley were called in and a sale prospectus was prepared. Before the

The imposing line-up of vats in the vat room (above).
André and Corinne Mentzelopoulos in 1980, the year
in which he was elected "Aquitain de l'année" (left).

contract was signed a firm offer arrived – from a willing buyer in France.

Just before Christmas they announced that a solution had been found, that the estate alone was to be sold, for 72 million francs, to one of the oldest french grocery chains, Félix Potin.

Ironically (and perhaps inevitably), the only man in France apparently willing to offer the Ginestets a reasonable and honourable deal, rather than to take advantage of their distress, was not French, but Greek. For the major shareholder in Félix Potin was André Mentzelopoulos. At the time of the purchase he was 62 years old, with an outstanding career behind him.

For some years Mentzelopoulos had been worried about the inflated prices being paid for property in Paris and had been looking for a major agricultural estate as an alternative means of investing in property, increasingly the best way of coping with the inevitable ravages of inflation. Moreover, he had known the Ginestets for some years – and, as a major shareholder in Vins Nicolas, largest and most famous of French retail wine merchants, he had more than a nodding acquaintance with the wine business.

Anyone who ever dealt with Mentzelopoulos has always remarked on the directness of his dealing technique and his painstaking obsession

One of the best and most significant plots of land on the estate – the Cap de Haut (above). A view down the L'allée du presbytére (left).

with detail, although he was able to act decisively when required. This it took only a few days for the two sides to agree the deal. Mentzelopoulos understood the Ginestets' feelings: they were battered, they felt that they had been treated like dirt by the French authorities and the French companies they had been dealing with; it was important for them to come out of the negotiations with their dignity and their self-esteem intact.

Nevertheless, the contrast between the two sides was complete. Mentzelopoulos was a charming man of considerable urbanity, dignity and thoughtfulness, with manners which seemed, if anything, over-formal and polite, yet he was nonetheless a pure financier. "My hobby is finance," he explained; his terms of reference were not really

The growth of the vine is secured with wicker, partly to allow a balance between greenery and grapes and partly for aesthetic reasons (top). It is, in part, the complex gravelly soil of the Puch Sem Peyre that gives the Cabernet Sauvignon its incomparable depth and concentration (below).

industrial at all. The Ginestets were not financially orientated: they were both deeply involved in the narrow world of Bordeaux.

But because Mentzelopoulos treated them as human beings, the deal was swiftly struck. He – or rather Félix Potin – was to buy the estate and it alone, for 72 million francs, of which 90 per cent was to be paid immediately, and the remainder in five years' time. At least it fulfilled the Ginestets' non-financial conditions: their family business was to enjoy the exclusive sale of the estate's wine for five years; Pierre was to live in the château for the rest of his life; and there was assurance of continuity of employment for the workers on the estate.

New, specially constructed clay drains, based on those used in the eighteenth century, have been laid in some areas of the estate (top).
According to how the growth is to be tied, a length of wicker is chosen from the bundle at the end of the row (below).

THE RENAISSANCE OF MARGAUX

For a proprietor who claimed that his hobby was financial management, André Mentzelopoulos saw little return from his investment in the few years between his purchase of the estate and his untimely death in 1980. He was fortunate in that the market for Bordeaux's wines was already improving at the time of his purchase: within a year he was able to recoup 12 million francs from the purchase price through sales of some of the three unsold vintages – 1974, 1975 and 1976 – included in the price of the estate. But these sales were over-shadowed by the massive investment programme he immediately undertook.

Margaux has now expanded into a major agri-cultural business; even in 1979, sales, though they were not swallowed by stock depletions, had increased to 12 million francs. The most impressive aspect of the changes is their sheer thoroughness. Seemingly, not a single pebble on this stony property was left unturned – and even though M. Mentzelopoulos surrounded himself with numerous high-powered advisers, the only change he made to the permanent staff on the estate was to bring in a new estate manager, Phillippe Barré, who had been running a large estate in Provence.

The changes started with the earth itself and what was planted on it. Part of Les Brauzes had a layer of clay removed; parcels of the Cap de Haut and the Puch Sem Peyre received new, specially made clay drains. The stream running down from the village between the Cap de Haut and the park

The traditional barriques used at Château Margaux are still made on the estate at the rate of two a day. The tonnellerie (above) and the different stages in the production of barriques (right).

*Three generations of maîtres de chai: Marcellus (top
left), Marcel (top right and below right) and Jean
Grangerou (below left).*
Traditional oak cuves with their copper fittings (right).

was thoroughly dredged; and the slope below the church and the cemetery – previously used largely as a rubbish dump – was cleared, filled with earth and planted with Cabernet Sauvignon. The programme initiated several years before by Jean-Pierre Blanchard changed several gears: under Barré's direction nearly 30 acres were replanted within four years. Two of the changes yard were just as sweeping. In 1980 M. Barré cleared the whole of the top of the Cap de Haut. This was immensely costly, for it involved leaving this precious part of the estate fallow for five years, then planting vines which would not produce grapes worthy of the *appellation* (let alone *le grand vin*) for five more years. It was the first time for over 70 years that this particular plot had

were fundamental: the lowest slopes of the Cap de Haut ('Les Bassanes'), which had always been devoted to the Sauvignon vines used to make "Pavillon Blanc" were replaced with Merlot. Conversely, the vines at Virefougasse were uprooted to make way for the Sauvignon Blanc needed for the new "Pavillon Blanc".

The changes in the historic heart of the vineyard been seen naked. Elsewhere on the estate, finding that the cattle on *Le Grand Barrail* could not produce the thousand tons or so of manure required annually by an estate for which chemical fertilizer would be risky, if not actually harmful, M. Mentzelopoulos bought the Ile Vincent, nearly 200 acres of pasture and woodland which borders *Le Grand Barrail* to the north.

The interior was imaginatively restored in the Second Empire style by Henri Samuel and Jean Feray, the Inspecteur Principal des Monuments Historiques. The boldness and flair with which the work was carried out generally disarm any criticism as to its appropriateness.

Laura Mentzelopoulos.

The first results of the new replanting showed up with the record vintage of 1979, which filled all 23 fermenting vats. Production in general increased very considerably during the 1980s; only a few more hectares of vines have been added, but the vineyard still corresponds almost exactly to the historic heart of the estate established three centuries ago. More significantly, the yields from the new vines are far greater than those from the older vines they replaced. An early indication of the future became apparent in 1980, when the wine produced in vast quantities from seven-year-old Merlot vines was deemed the best on the estate by the men who made the wine.

The judgement was the combined result of innate inherited experience, and a more scientific palate, the former provided by Jean Grangerou, *maître de chai* since his father had retired ten years before, and the latter by Professor Emile Peynaud, retired director of Bordeaux's *Institut Oenologique*. Peynaud, the first man to explain secondary or malolactic fermentation scientifically, was a natural choice for a new proprietor anxious to surround himself with the best advice available. The team proved its competence by making a good wine in 1977 – a year in which the Merlot failed. And in 1978, for the first time in many years, Margaux was widely acclaimed as having produced perhaps the outstanding wine of the year.

The corollary to the replanting process was a major investment in new *chais*. Starting with the 1980 vintage, the whole process of making and storing the considerable and increasing quantities of white wine sold as "Pavillon Blanc" was transferred to the *chais* at Château Abel Laurent. There the most modern fermenting vats and cooling equipment were installed in a totally air-conditioned *chai*. It was Professor Peynaud who instigated the changes. The 1978 white wine – deep, profoundly fruity – persuaded him that it could be worth many times the mere eight francs a bottle at which the Ginestets had sold it wholesale. Now, 12 years later, it is firmly ensconced in its rightful place as one of the great white wines of the Gironde. Yet it breaks all the rules: not only is it made in the Médoc (rather than the Graves, source of all Bordeaux's other great dry whites), it is a wine which matures superbly despite being made exclusively from the Sauvignon Blanc.

The investments planned by the new owner made sense only if seen as a long-term strategy for making Margaux into a far more productive agricultural business than ever before. The new vines may be more productive, but quality has been dramatically and regularly improved by a policy of severe selectivity, of which a foretaste was provided by M. Grangerou's decision to allow only half the 1974 vintage to be sold as *grand vin*. Such a policy implies the facilities to produce, bottle, store – and sell – relatively large quantities of the "Pavillons Rouge" and "Blanc". For the wine set aside by M. Grangerou was used to resurrect a brand not seen for half a century, although as a matter of policy the 1974 "Pavillon Rouge" was not put on the market until 1980. By then it was a relatively mature wine – hence the need for extensive storage facilities.

Although the bulk of money being spent on the estate went into the vineyard and winery, the most spectacular changes concern its non-productive face: the gentleman's residence and its immediate surroundings. Here again, the changes have been the most profound in the 170 years since the château was first constructed.

The easiest, though not the least expensive, part of the thorough job of restoration concerned the exterior of the château. It was simply cleaned, its stones replaced where necessary and its decorations revealed, the work supervised by M. Mastorakis, France's *Architecte en Chef des Monuments Historiques*. But it required real flair to order the removal of the many accumulated coats of paint which concealed the pure, narrow arches which form the ceiling of the entrance hall behind the château's *porte-cochère*. The hall, although surrounded simply by the kitchen and other domestic offices, now has an unmistakable dignity and grandeur, like the entrance porch of a fine church.

A similar emphasis on bringing out the purity of line which distinguishes so much of Combes' work is evident throughout the interior of the house. It was precisely these rooms, on the *rez-de-chaussée* at the head of the main staircase and the floor above, that posed the biggest problems for Jean Feray, *Inspecteur Principal des Monuments Historiques,* who was responsible for the château's interior, and another leading French government expert, Henri Samuel, who was

The exterior of the château and its immediate surroundings were completely restored and cleaned when André Mentzelopoulos turned his attention to the non-productive side of Château Margaux (right).

responsible for the furnishings. For the first time that the château had been furnished was several decades after the house had been built, by the Aguados, when taste was very different from that prevailing under the first Napoléon. Moreover, the original schema had been more or less retained and restored by the Ginestets.

formal, as the exterior would suggest. The house is only 55 feet (17 metres) from front to back, and because the house is two rooms deep, none of them seems too overwhelming in dimensions. In the entrance hall the two niches in which Combes had envisaged statues of Achilles now contain busts of Roman Emperors. Behind the hall lie the

The choice was either to complete the Ginestets' work, or to be bold and return to an imaginative reconstruction of the interior as it would have been, if it had been completed at the same time as the exterior. The latter won.

Yet the interior of Margaux is not as grand, or as

three reception rooms, none overwhelmingly large, none unsuited to normal family life. To the left is the dining-room, redecorated in rather pompous *faux-marbe*. Its magnificent Egyptian-style stove, formerly blackened, has been cleaned and revealed in its original terra-cotta colour.

The magnificent Egyptian-style stove in the dining room, formerly blackened, has been meticulously restored to its original pale terracotta (left). In the entrance hall (above left) grandeur is tempered by purity of line. A niche in which the architect, Louis Combes, had envisaged a statue of Achilles now contains a bust of a Roman Emperor (above right).

Many original pieces were incorporated into the decorative scheme, including books belonging to Alexandre Aguado. Corinne Mentzelopoulos has added a number of fine items, like a music cabinet (top right), which was presented to General Murat by Napoleon after his victory at the Pyramids. Other fittings (right) have been chosen in keeping with the style.

Directly behind the hall is the library, all in green, and to its right, nearest the river, is the *salon* – all lightness in a warm praline colour.

Immediately above the hall is the main drawing-room. And it is on this floor that the decorator's imagination ran riot. Where purity is the essential feature of the decoration and furnishings of the floor below, the drawing-room is magnificently, extravagantly pink, with a bold vinous motif on every surface and object. The main bedroom directly above the library is decorated in an equally bold and successful Chinese style.

Outside the château the task was somewhat easier, once one of France's most distinguished landscape architects, M. Loup de Viane, had thought through the implications of the date of the château's construction. The taste of the First Empire, so noticeable in the Egyptian touches – the sphinxes at the bottom of the main staircase, the delicious patterns on the great stove in the dinning-room – was matched by an equal craze for "Englishness" in the designs of gardens. This word spells informality to the French, and, at the time, was combined with the use of magnolias and camellias en masse as the basis for the outline of a garden. So Loup de Viane did away with the formal, patterned flower-beds which surrounded the house on two sides. He girdled the house with crisp white gravel, itself framed in a single massive lawn around three sides of the house, and arranged a mass of camellias and magnolias on and around the green grass. This artful informality, evident also in the interior decoration of the house, suits it perfectly. It sweeps away the false pretence of Margaux as a royal palace, and transforms it into an elegantly formal, yet, just as it is inside, a highly liveable-in home, surrounded by grass to stroll on and paths through (carefully thinned) beechwoods with vistas to distant vines.

Inevitably, the sudden death of André Mentzelopoulos at the end of 1980 was perceived by the ever-gossiping Bordeaux wine community in a very different way from the family. The estate, it was generally agreed, would be sold and sooner rather than later.

Mother and daughter were at one in seeing things completely differently. Their determination to carry on became clear within a few weeks: "My father died on the 10th December", Corinne Mentzelopoulos told me, "and on the 15th my mother and I went to Margaux where we assembled the estate workers to reassure them. We weren't sure of ourselves, far from it, but we had to give the impression that we knew what we were going to do. At first we continued my fathers' work out of simple pride, love of Margaux and for my father's memory, because we simply didn't have the right to let it fall".

For two years mother and daughter worked amicably together, not only at the technical level on the estate but in promoting the wine and the image of the château. They were natural stars on both sides of the Atlantic. They featured, not only in numerous television programmes, but in virtually every magazine devoted to wine, attracting awards from a number of reputable specialist magazines like *Decanter* and *Alles Über Wein*.

Two years after her husband's death, Laura remarried. She started to spend most of the year in New York with her new husband but continued to promote the family wine, especially in the

Detail of a gilded bronze chandelier.

United States. Since then, mother and daughter have combined occasionally to create events at Margaux worthy of the magnificence of the setting. Most spectacular was the *fête* mounted in 1984 to celebrate the fiftieth anniversary of the end of Prohibition in the United States.

When her mother remarried, Corinne took over the responsibility of running the estate. This did not stop the rumours that the estate was for sale. But from the start her position has been clear: "Of course we could sell the estate, but what would I do for the rest of my life? I could always find another occupation, but I could never find another Margaux to love and cherish. I could never find another challenge like Margaux, where every vintage presents new opportunities, new problems, in the never-ending search for perfection. For Margaux is not like any normal business: you can't simply decide on a new product, on new packaging, a new taste. We're not even wine-makers here, we're merely the servants of a *terroir,* enabling it to express its finest qualities. Margaux is eternal, and you're only part of a chain which stretches back and forward over centuries. You're the guardian of an extraordinary *terroir* and of the historic building which celebrate its glories. In everything you do you have to have both eyes fixed on this extra, historic dimension."

Corinne may perceive herself as a simple servant of an historic tradition. But fortunately she was born to be a great wine-maker. She is truly her father's daughter in her intelligence, her sharpness, her dogged, determined character, her love of detail which amounts to obsessional con-

cern which is the common characteristic of the great wine-maker the world over – for wine-making is a relatively simple business in which attention to every little detail is crucial to success.

Corinne's policy has been perfectly straightforward. She has tried to "run Margaux like a family business. We needed regularity after having re-established the good name of the wine. One must always be aware of the judgement of posterity. Above all one must have in mind the words of Marshal Lyautey: 'When you do not strain every nerve to be the first you do not fall into second place but inevitably become the last'".

Her work is divided into two parts: continuing the many projects left unfinished by her father's untimely death, works which took up most of the first half of the 1980s; and undertaking tasks which her father had never envisaged and going even further in improving the quality of the wine. She had a difficult act to follow as her father, before his death, had drawn up complete and detailed plans for the rebuilding of the "winery". The refurbishment of the château had been so spectacular and well-publicized that it rather threw into shadow the even more important work, which extended for over a decade after the takeover, of transforming the whole network of working buildings. These buildings had formed an integral part of Combes' Palladian vision – a vision in which the elegance of the owners' château was consciously reflected in the buildings from which they derived their wealth.

Given the unity and completeness of Combes' plan, it was unthinkable to build anything new

Entrance to the vat room.

above ground. This greatly complicated André Mentzelopoulos's biggest single project, the new *chai* for the second-year wine. Although Margaux's main *chai,* is the most famous and, historically, the most spectacular in the Médoc, yet it can accommodate only one year's production.

So a new *chai* was needed and one, moreover, which combined a number of apparently conflicting requirements. Corinne was always aware, as she says, that "we find ourselves inevitably on the thin edge of tradition and innovation". In this case the edge was razor-sharp. The new *chai* had to be totally invisible, and built between harvests, yet it had to be big enough to contain more than one vintage in cask – for the château, ever-conscious of the new-found reputation for the wine's sturdiness and longevity, now tends to bottle its wines after a full two years in wood. The *chai* also had to house a bottling line, and several hundred thousand bottles.

The local architect, Maziéres, triumphantly succeeded in resolving the dilemma – and, moreover, ensuring that it was built in a mere ten months after the 1981 harvest had been safely gathered in. The new *chai* was created by excavating a huge hole directly in front of the *cours du cuvier,* in place of the car park. It involved removing a mere four rows of vines and its covering, a neatly tended grass sward, serves to insulate the *chai* beneath; the temperature barely alters throughout the year, even without air conditioning. It's the first underground *chai* in the Médoc and a major technical achievement. Because it is below the water table, for instance, two pumps are permanently employed to remove the water. Furthermore, the whole works – not only as a machine

Restoration work has not been restricted to the château and the chais. Extensive work has been carried out around La Cour des chais, the vat room (above and top right) and la salle des vendangeurs including re-roofing, rebuilding the floor and restoring the exteriors to their original condition.

for storing, bottling and despatching wine, but as a worthy contribution to Margaux as the grandest of all agricultural enterprises.

The same theme, of improvement and modernization concealed at great expense, continues in the estate's two major "working" courtyards. While the vats were being modernized so were the *fouloirs egrappoirs* which de-stem the grapes as they arrive from the vineyard. The grapes are now tipped into shallow troughs, rather like trays lined with granite, to facilitate a final inspection before they are transformed into wine. The yard itself was re-paved, the previously rather tacky reception centre refurbished, a small, discreet tasting room tucked in between it and the vats.

More spectacular was the refurbishment of the *cour des artisans,* to the left between the château and the church, where tractors now fit snugly into converted bays designed for horse-drawn agricultural implements – with maintenance bays discreetly hidden.

But, however long, complicated and spectacular these changes, they had all been foreseen by André Mentzelopoulos. Only after the new *chai* had been finished, and the 1982 vintage harvested, did the daughter step out from her father's footsteps. He had refused to allow stainless steel vats to replace the lovely wooden vats which had formed part of Margaux's history. In fact the new wine-makers discovered that fermentation in wood carried with it a number of advantages if, as at Margaux, the vats were regularly renewed and the cooling apparatus modernized. But the vats were barely big enough for the enormous 1982 vintage and since then Corinne has discreetly installed twelve stainless steel fermentation vats, each holding 185 hectolitres of wine, a significant increase of capacity, since the 26 existing wooden vats each hold only 150 hectolitres – and are still enough for most vintages.

In 1983 Corinne took another major initiative: taking on a new *regisseur,* destined to work with and then succeed Philip Barre, who was approaching retirement age. Her choice, Paul Pontallier, startled the Médoc, not only because of his youth (he was 27 when he was appointed), but also because of his inexperience – he had never run an estate in France. The son and grandson of winegrowers, he had been recognized as the most brilliant pupil of his generation at the Oenological school at Bordeaux and had worked in Chile to gain experience. Corinne's explanation of her choice is simple. "I wanted someone of my own age with whom I could work for a long time".

Once the wine-making has been perfected, attention turned back to the vineyard – in doing so she was setting a trend now being followed by many of the most distinguished wine-makers in the Gironde. In November 1986 she brought together the owners of the eight estates now generally regarded as First Growths (the historic five plus Ausone, Petrus and Cheval Blanc) to work together on their common viticultural problems in collaboration with the official researchers who had already minutely examined every parcel in Margaux's own vineyard.

At the estate the family has already made a

Paul Pontallier (above) succeeded Philippe Barré as régisseur in 1983.

major contribution by allowing their technical team to delay picking the grapes until up to a week later than any of their neighbours, allowing the grapes to develop more concentration. This end can be further achieved by pruning excessively large bunches of grapes in July; a technique Corinne learnt from Christian Mouiex at the meticulously tended Château Petrus.

Five years earlier she had given a lecture at the second annual Seminar for Wine Professionals in New York in which she summed up the principles which underlay her commercial policy: to recreate a "spontaneous" demand for the wine based on its undeniable quality; to be available in all the major markets; to recapture Margaux's position on the wine lists of the world's major restaurants; to produce great – or at least excellent – wine every year; and to create an indissoluble link between Margaux and the family which owned it. True to her stubborn and persistent character, no-one can say that she has not carried out her policy.

The determination and vision of Corinne Mentzelopoulos (above) cannot be underestimated in ensuring the continued quality of Château Margaux. Following double page: Some of the finest bottles from the cellar.

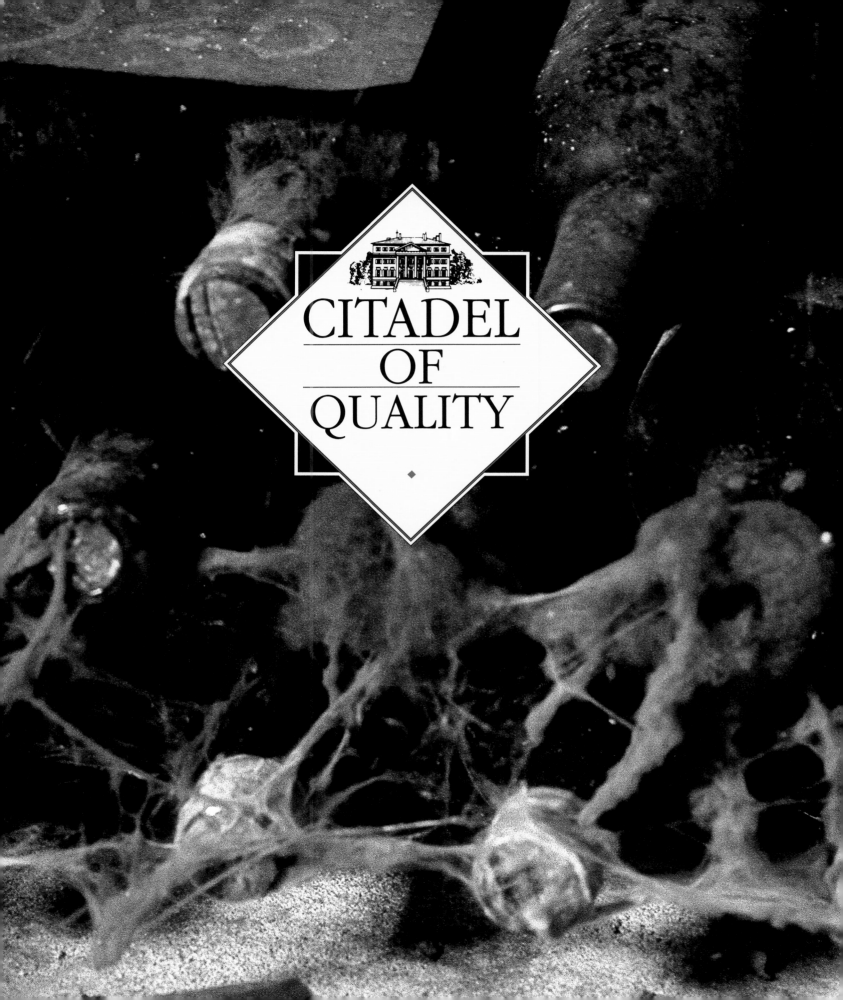

CITADEL
OF
QUALITY

Were it not for the accidents of geology and geography, Margaux would be merely a village as anonymous as many of the others scattered along the 60 miles of the Médoc peninsula between the Bay of Biscay and the broad estuary of the Gironde. Its place in non-vinous history is pretty minimal. A considerable hoard of Bronze Age relics was, indeed, found near the village. But this "*Trésor de Margaux*" (now in a Bordeaux museum) is not, in itself, proof of any importance it might have possessed at the time.

There is a possibility that it was the site in late Roman times of *Thermae Mariolicae,* one of the many villas owned by the Roman poet Ausonius, who gave his name to Château Ausone in St-Emillion and whose villas are claimed with greater or lesser justification by many villages scattered around the Gironde. The theory that Margaux was so blessed has been put forward by Bernard Ginestet. He believes that the site of the villa was at La Fontanelle, at the north-eastern edge of the estate nearest the river.

However, Margaux remained a relative backwater until the early eighteenth century. Then the first stage of a new royal post-road to Paris was built from Bordeaux to the historic – and actual – ferry port of Lamarque, and Margaux gained a posting-inn (which is still standing, set back from the present main road) and the privilege of sending letters every day. But all this is subordinate to the vine: and it is the château's historic name "*La Mothe de Margaux*", the mound of hill of Margaux, which gives the first clue to its major distinctive asset. For the great wines of the Médoc are invariably grown on the most prominent of the gravel slopes to the west of the Gironde estuary; these form low rounded elevations.

The geological processes which created these sanctuaries for the vine were so tortuous that their is no uniformity between the various ridges. For the Gironde is the confluence of two major river systems, the Garonne which originates in the Pyrenees some hundreds of miles to the south, and the Dordogne which flows west from the Massif Central. Something over a million years ago, the waters carved out the bed of the river from the chalky limestone. Subsequently successive waves of rock pounded into gravel, and stones washed down from the mountains formed layer upon irregular layer on the old bed of the river. The disturbances were enormous – the gravel has been traced down to over 100 feet below the present bed of the river, and the gravel layers are over 300 feet above it at some places south of Bordeaux. The process was continuous over half a million years or more: rock was deposited, then scoured out so that all regularity was destroyed. Geologically, the rocks were largely deposited during the Gunzien era around 800,000 years ago; the shaping was achieved mainly 400,000 years later during the Mindelian period.

Finally, the whole area west from the gravel ridges was covered with a thick layer of sand, which provides the soil for the pine forests and the long white beaches and immense sand dunes of the Landes which cover the whole western two-thirds of the Médoc peninsula. The result

Vines have been grown on the gravelly soils around the château for many centuries – traditional procedures, such as harvesting the grapes by hand, are still employed today (left).
This bottle (above), labelled as a sample, contains wine set aside for tasting before the assemblage.

Petit Verdot, Merlot, Cabernet Franc and Cabernet Sauvignon are the four grape varieties which together produce the subtle, elegant wines of Château Margaux. The Merlot (opposite, left), Sauvignon-Blanc (opposite, right). The latter is the grape of Pavillon Blanc.

could not have been better designed by a beneficient wine-loving deity. Climactically the area was ideal for the growing of the finest wines, which prefer the outer limits of the regions where the vine can be grown. The forests of the Landes protected the valley of the Gironde; the river itself provided

Nevertheless, great wine is made on only two of the major deposits of gravel, though both of them are intersected with numerous *jalles* or streams which separate individual communes (or, sometimes, individual estates). To the north are the ridges on which are perched St-Estèphe, Pauillac

further protection from the unexpected late frosts which are still a bane of Bordeaux; and the very variety of the thickness of the gravel banks, their composition, and the sub-soil on which they were superimposed further ensured that the wines of the Médoc would not be boringly uniform.

and St-Julien-Beychevelle. And to the south, in and around Margaux, we have, in the words of Professor Enjalbert "more than 20 classed growths within one of the historic citadels of quality" in the Médoc. The Professor's "citadel" is long, stretching for about four miles from the last

Burning the shoots after pruning (above and top left).
Maintenance to stakes and training wires is also
carried out in winter (below left).

northern ridge of Soussans, through Margaux to Cantenac to the south – with a further outcrop at Labarde. But it is also narrow, not much more than a mile wide, for it is sandwiched between the rich alluvial meadows (*palus*) on the banks of the Gironde and the sand advancing in irregular fingers from Landes. As usual in the Médoc, there are a few outcrops to the west, in this case particularly at Château du Tertre in Arsac.

There are few of the large stones so obvious in the north: by contrast, the total percentage of stony matter is higher in and around Margaux. The soil is simply thinner. Of course the smaller the stones, and the higher the proportion they represent of the total soil, the better the drainage. In this respect Margaux has another advantage over its northern brethren, since the sub-soil tends to be chalkier, containing more of the original

basic limestone of the region than they do (indeed the shore of the Gironde opposite Margaux shows some veritable chalk cliffs around Blaye). And this again improves the drainage, although the "*mothe*" of Margaux has slopes gentler than "*La Fite*" and "*La Mothe*" up in Pauillac. So virtually the whole commune is, in theory, capable of producing fine wine.

But the poverty and permeability of both surface and sub-soil throw into even greater relief the problems encountered with a patch of ground where the percentage of clayey, impermeable material is too great to permit proper drainage. Once the roots of the vine encounter such a layer, once the plants start to absorb too much moisture from roots too near the surface, then their grapes become dangerous impurities in any wine of quality.

Such problems can be eliminated: shortly after

The changing face of Margaux. Throughout the seasons the vines are subject to the vagaries of the Médocain weather (above).
(Right): After the harvest the leaves redden and fall symbolizing another year-end in the life cycle of Château Margaux.

buying Margaux, the late André Mentzelopoulos removed a layer of clay, over a foot thick, from an otherwise choice piece of ground (*Les Brauzes*) opposite Château Palmer. So strict are the regulations surrounding wines of such quality, that the clay this removed can be replaced only by earth from a similar piece of ground on the estate.

Nevertheless, such is the subtlety of the balance of nature in the Médoc that the soils of the best growths contain slightly more clay – even in the top three feet of soil – than less blessed plots. When M. Seguin analysed some of these soils he found only a slightly higher proportion of clay (an eighth instead of a twelfth), but, above all, far stonier ground: three-fifths of the top three feet were pebbles or gravel in the best *crus*, against a

third to two-fifths in the less distinguished ones.

If the soil is a crucially important element and the sub-soil scarcely less so, there is yet a third factor in the equation: the outlook enjoyed by any particular piece of ground. "For the wine to be good, the vines ought to be able to see the river and not be more than a kilometre away from it" is one of those old wives' tales which modern science has painstakingly proved to be extremely sound. The gravel banks tend to be at their thickest at the point where they meet the alluvial soil of the river banks. If slopes lead more or less directly into the river, then their drainage will tend to be better than average. This factor is

seemingly more important in Margaux than it is further north, where many of the finest wines are made from grapes grown on slopes which are on the second ridges, like those at Lafite and Mouton.

But all of the best slopes, however far from the river, face east or north-east. Thus the grapes will be steadily warmed by the rising sun, and as the evening shadows lengthen the daily cooling process will not be too abrupt. In addition to this, vines facing the river are less likely to suffer from damagingly late frosts than their inland equivalents, some of which are in veritable "frost pockets" in the woods.

The combination required is, therefore, a difficult one: the soil must be poor and stony, so that the roots have to dig for their moisture and such meagre nourishment as they can get down to perhaps 15 or 20 feet, so that the relatively few grapes they produce will have distilled the water they absorb into grape juice full of flavour – even before man gets to work on the fermentation process. The fields must be well-drained, and preferably face the river. Needless to say, the bulk of the Margaux vineyard fulfils most of these requirements. Indeed, looking at a map, it becomes immediately apparent why it is so far ahead of its fellow estates even in Margaux, a commune thickly spotted with growths blessed in 1855 – with five second growths, nine out of the then fourteen third growths and four fourth growths, all squashed into a "citadel" in Margaux, Cantenac, Labarde and Arsac.

But only Château Margaux had the bulk of its vines in major holdings on the "richer" slopes – for quality that is, though agriculturally they were the very reverse. Moreover, more as a matter of historical luck than vinous judgement, the château inherited a uniquely complex mixture of soils, which provides another reason for its supremacy. The "beating heart" of the vineyards lies in the two holdings mentioned in the first chapter. As is usual in historically well-settled landscapes, these two groups of fields have names which bear witness to the qualities locally associated with them.

Outside the estate's wall lies the Puch Sem Peyre – the local Gascon equivalent of the French *puits sans pierre* – well without stones. ("Parempuyre", a village at the Bordeaux end of the Médoc, has a name clearly derived from the same phenomenon.) These are eloquent names recognizing that the fields were so stony that you

The estate has its own herd of cattle to provide the vines with the manure they need.

could dig a well there without artificially reinforcing its walls with additional stones. Inside the wall the Cap de Haut – the high point – (locally pronounced Cadeo) slopes down to the stream which leads from the centre of the village down to the river. The names point up the salient aspects – their slopes and their stoniness – geographically associated with them. These qualities are of inestimable vinous value. Of course the estate has, historically, always owned other excellent holdings, some scattered on slopes well away from the river, notably on the other side of the château; but these two, which are roughly equal in size, account for nearly half the 170 or so acres of vines in the main part of the vineyard.

There is, however, a paradox in the names. Although the Cap de Haut looms above the château and its surrounding wood and park, it lies below the Puch Sem Peyre.

But it is the Cap de Haut, in particular, which provides the major explanation for the unique flavours and essences of the estate's wine – as opposed to its generally high quality. The special characters of wines in the Médoc may be fundamentally determined by the soil they grow in and the aspect they command, but the choice of varieties of grape also plays a crucial role. The basic variety is, of course, the Cabernet Sauvignon, tough and tannic, often reinforced by the Petit Verdot and by a little of the less colourful Cabernet Franc. Finesse and subtlety are provided by a very little Malbec and, to a much greater extent, by the Merlot, which is as universally dominant in Pomerol and St-Emilion as the Cabernet Sauvignon is in the Médoc. Every estate trots out the various percentages of each variety it

In the parcel of land, Les Platanes, in front of the château, harvesting by hand ensures an exceptionally high level of quality control.

*The rigorous standards applied to the gathering and
selection of grapes are similar to those established in the
late seventeenth century by Berlon. After the grapes
have been loaded into a hopper (right) they are taken
to the vat room where a further selection takes place
(top and above left). The discarded woody matter
(above right) is spread on the vineyard.*

has in the vineyard. But none of these can ever be exact: if you take the percentages by acreage, then you will be counting young vines (whose produce cannot, by all, be included in the estate's "*grand vin*") and old ones (which may be producing a very small crop, but are kept because of the high quality of their few grapes). If you take the quantities harvested, then only the men actu-

new vines were planted.

Margaux, in theory, falls somewhere between Latour and Mouton-Rothschild (overwhelmingly – 75 per cent or more – composed of Cabernet Sauvignon) and Lafite, traditionally strong in Merlot. At the moment, roughly 75 per cent of the Margaux vineyard is planted with Cabernet Sauvignon, just under 25 per cent with Merlot,

ally responsible for making the wine know the exact make-up of the year's total vintage or (which may be very different) of the percentages of different varieties in the *grand vin*. These may vary considerably over the years (although, of course, the *maître de chai* always wants to maintain a stable "style"). These percentages are especially misleading in a vineyard like Margaux, where there was a great deal of replanting in the 1970s after a decade or more in which very few

just under five per cent with Petit Verdot (much of it over 60 years old and therefore not very productive) with a pinch of Cabernet Franc tucked away on the road just beyond the Puch Sem Peyre – though these proportions themselves conceal the admixture of different varieties within many of the older fields. Nevertheless, Margaux is now trying to ensure a rigid separation of varieties in different parts of the vineyard.

But the proportions are very different in the Cap

A great spirit of camaraderie grows up amongst the vendangeurs as they work together, share their meals and drink the fruits of their labour.

*A high percentage of the 200 or so vendangeurs come
back to the château year after year. Their familiarity
with the vineyard enables them to make a more
informed selection.*

de Haut, where all the lower slopes are planted with Merlot, which accounts for well over half the total. The explanation is obvious if you look at the soil: at quite a specific point on the slope the soil gets decidedly whiter, indicating that the "dirty limestone" is peeking through the outcrops of gravel, and below that point – on *la terre blanche,* "the white soil" – the Merlot flourishes. This is vital

through, the quality of Margaux suffered, since its uniqueness was based so firmly on the high proportion of Merlot in its best plots.

So, in the past, Margaux required a perfect year – like 1870, 1900 or 1961 – to show itself at its glorious best. But the balance was always thought to be fragile: the soils are so many and varied, the Merlot so touchy in the Cap de Haut, that nature

for the particular elegance and delicate fruitiness of the wine. It is the Merlot which contributes the "blackcurrant" bouquet to the wines of Pomerol and St-Emilion, but it is particularly susceptible to *pourriture* (rot) in years when the summer is unusually wet, invariably a bad sign for the quality of the vintage. In the past, in mediocre or bad years, when a château like Latour can rely on the solidity of the Cabernet Sauvignon to see it

was seemingly jealous, inclined to ration Margaux's best years and thus increase appreciation of them. Of course, the problems of producing a great wine in less-than-perfect years can be overcome, but only at the cost of rigorous and costly discipline which may reduce very considerably the yield of wine deemed worthy of the label "Château Margaux". But this traditional view has been completely overturned in the years since

The wine is "racked" off the gross lees, or sediment,
every few months – the open basin allows the wine to
aerate.

André Mentzelopoulos bought the estate. The detailed attention paid to every stage of the wine-making process, together with a ruthless division of wines between the "Grand Vin" and the second wine, the Pavillon Rouge, has resulted in a complete reclassification of the estate's wines. No longer are they a by-word for their feminine charm, their unreliability, their success only in the

best years. Instead they have become, in a sense, the commune's answer to Latour, sturdy wines, long to mature, reliable even in light years, but retaining the velvety, the rich truffly earthiness of the "historic" Margaux.

Tasted ten years later, indeed, the 1978 Grand Vin, the first great year *"signé"* André Mentzelopoulos, was less developed, far dumber,

more powerful than the Latour, traditionally the slowest to mature of all the First Growths. The 1978 was no accident: the qualities of the "new" Margaux emerged clearly in several subsequent vintages, notably the 1983, the 1988, and, above all, the 1986, considered by many (including Professor Peynaud) to be one of the greatest wines made in the Médoc since the historic 1961s.

This transformation, which is largely a revelation of qualities which were inherent in the wine but hidden by decades of sloppy wine-making and lack of selectivity, would not have surprised the great William Lawton. In 1815 this all-powerful winebroker wrote down his impressions of the wines of Bordeaux, a document generally taken as gospel. In this memo he wrote of the wines of the commune as being noted for "their firmness, which sometimes one could call hardness, which distinguishes them from those of Saint Julien and Pauillac – which – principally those of Saint Julien – are more noted for their softness and suavity". These remarks fit in very well with the qualities of the "new" Margaux, which thus emerges as a reversion to an older tradition.

The idea of an overriding "communal" style seems to me somewhat overdone. Even the supposedly homogenous St-Julien is clearly divided into two halves by the village of St-Julien, while Pauillac covers two totally different vineyards: the southern estates, like Latour and the two Pichons, are next door to Léoville Lascases, which are separated only by a small stream (*"jalle"*) while they are two miles (and the substantial town of Pauillac) away from Pauillac Nord, remarkable for two great wines, Lafite and Mouton, which themselves could not be more dissimilar.

And yet the old differences remain. In vintages which, though considered fine, like 1982 and 1989, are relatively rich and soft, lacking in a general firmness, the Southern Médoc as a whole does not show at its best. In these vintages the Château Margaux, though undoubtedly superior to any other wine from the region, still shares their general attributes – thus the 1983 Margaux is generally thought better than the 1982, a reversal of the general reputation of the other First Growths.

Because of the homogeny of its holdings it is not surprising that within the commune of Margaux,

The process of remontage is essential in allowing the colour of the wine to develop.

the château is almost alone in the potential quality of its wine; the only potential competitor is its immediate neighbour to the south, with sunny slopes lying side by side with some of Margaux's finest acreage: Château Palmer.

But historically Palmer has been less lucky than Margaux. It was only separated from Château d'Issan in the last half of the eighteenth century. And although the legend says otherwise, it was not a major force before the Revolution. Indeed, it only acquired its present name in the early nineteenth century, when one of Wellington's generals, arriving in Bordeaux as part of the triumphal British army after the Peninsular War, took a fancy to it. Moreover, at the crucial time of the 1855 classification, the estate was being reorganized. So it is only a third growth, even though some of its *terroir* is the equal of parts of Margaux, and for a few years during the late 1960s and early 1970s it was making wine better than that made by Margaux. But the advantage was necessarily temporary and in the 1980s Palmer has retreated into the shadow of its "nobler" neighbour.

This point about "luck" is an important one, for a key note of success in the Médoc is to have had a compact holding of suitable soil. And none of the other estates in the commune – not even Palmer – seems to have been blessed with this attribute with any consistency. For the village of Margaux is a curious one. It is small, varying between 800 and 1500 inhabitants over the centuries. Nevertheless it has, historically, been divided into a series of definite *quartiers* each clustered around one of the major châteaux, Lascombes, Durfort-Vivens, and so on. But this in turn led to a complicated patchwork of holdings among the major landowners who dominated the village. Where other communes – the case of St-Julien is an obvious one – consisted of quite distinct châteaux, each at the centre of its own vineyard and with the bulk of its holdings clearly delineated, the land map of Margaux is a nightmare. Even Margaux itself it not exempt: there are odd holdings belonging, seemingly, to half the village. But it is a compact estate, with its two major holdings, each as big as many famous Médocain vineyards. Moreover, even the holdings not within the heart of the estate – notably at Chigarail, Les Ninottes and Virefougasse – have

been owned by the estate for several hundred years and have amply proved their capacity to produce fine wines over the centuries.

By contrast virtually every other estate in the village has, historically, been fragmented. There has been an incredibly tangled vine-go-round over the past century and a half, between the two parts of the Rauzan estate, Malescot St-Exupéry,

Malesme-Becker, Durfort-Vivens – not to mention the parcelling up of the now virtually defunct third growth Desmirail. The intermingling has meant that none of them could establish the sort of settled reputation available to major growths elsewhere in the Médoc. Recently, of course, the expansion of the Lascombes estate, after its purchase in the early 1950s by a syndicate of

(Above and left): Wine is pumped over the surface of the cap of solids which has floated to the surface, and is pushed down with wooden poles. One of the skills of the wine-maker is in guaging how many times the remontage must be carried out.

103

The main chai, where the first year's wines are stored (top), is the most famous and spectacular in the Médoc. The underground chai, built in 1982, accomodates the second year's wines (below). It is the tradition of maturing Château Margaux in oak barriques that helps to create these unique wines (right).

Le maître de chai, Jean Grangerou, inspecting and tasting "Pavillon Blanc" during its fermentation.

Americans headed by Alexis Lichine, has created one of the biggest estates in the Médoc. Nevertheless, even the most fervent admirers of this distinguished second growth would not seriously compare it with Margaux. In fact only 50 of Lascombes' 200 acres of vines are really worthy of a second growth.

So Château Margaux was well-placed to be the central redoubt in the "citadel of quality". It was thrice blessed, with the name of the commune itself, through its *terroir* and through its relatively homogeneous character.

The new managers are fully aware of the estate's uniqueness, its potential – and the limited degree of influence they have over it. In the words of Paul Pontallier, "the myth of Margaux develops outside our control and we have no power over it. On the contrary, when people come here, we try and remove the mystery, we show them what we have done openly: we show them that a great wine comes from a specific piece of earth and a lot of hard work. A great wine is not simply a gift of the Holy Ghost. It comes from a piece of soil which has perhaps been blessed by the gods, but in any case has been chosen, assembled, worked on by the hand of man over the centuries. And in the case of Margaux we are talking of parcels of land brought together between the thirteenth and seventeenth centuries".

Man can nevertheless above all select and refine, for perhaps the single most important key to improving the quality of the wine of any estate is to reduce the production, first by pruning as severely as possible, a procedure normal in all estates, but also by eliminating some of the wine from the Grand Vin (although it would be wrong to go along with the old assumption that the production of fine wine automatically requires low yields. In some years (like 1970, 1982 and 1989) both yield and quality were high).

Selection is also crucial even in the best years – and above all in years like 1989 when there is a danger of dilution through (relative) overproduction, or 1987 when some of the grapes may not have been completely ripe. As we saw, the selection process had started in Margaux in 1912 by the creation Pavillon Rouge as a second label, but was abandoned at Margaux – as everywhere else

in the Médoc – during the dire years of the 1930s.

It was first systematically resurrected at Latour, when its purchase by British financial interests in 1962 was soon followed by the creation of Les Forts de Latour. Its extension to Margaux was foreshadowed when Jean Grangerou, on his own initiative, declassified half the miserable 1874 vintage, a policy enthusiastically followed and refined under the Mentzelopoulos family.

For them the recreation of Pavillon Rouge was only a first step. In 1978-79 it accounted for only a quarter or so of the total production. It gradually increased to around half, and in 1987, when conscientious estates like Margaux preserved their reputation for making fine wine in a bad year by eliminating over half their production, Margaux produced a fine, elegant Grand Vin by declassify-

ing a full 60 per cent of the total. Indeed the equivalent of 60,000 bottles was completely discarded and the wine sold as anonymous Appellation Controlée Margaux – the château did not follow the example of Latour (and, lately, of Lafite as well) of selling a third wine, a generic commune wine, but one graced with the name of the château.

The efforts made at Margaux were not in vain. During the 1980s, in Robert Parker's words, "Margaux has become the wine of reference. I did not believe that the estate could surpass the sublime wines produced in 1982 and 1983. Yet the 1984 was one of their best years and the 1986 is likely to be at least as extraordinary as the 1982 and 1983. Indeed it could become the perfect

Le maître de chai's office is situated in the middle of the vat room.

*The cellar houses some of the château's most celebrated
vintages. The oldest date from the nineteenth century.
Asked to define his idea of happiness, Friedrich Engels
replied: "Château Margaux 1848".*

Margaux of our dreams. It is already legendary, what with its fruity characteristics, its penetrating aromas, and its extraordinary length".

But even these encomiums are not enough for the new team. Part of the new concentration on the vineyard rather than the wine-making and Margaux is in the forefront of the resulting initiatives. These are inevitably long-term. At Margaux they wait five years after uprooting vines before replanting, and the new vines will not be making wine worthy of the Grand Vin for at least eight years more. So it requires a good deal of confidence in the need for change to behave like Paul Pontallier. He is restoring the historic balance of grape varieties by planting more Petit Verdot.

It is an old variety, much esteemed in the past for the strength, the fruitiness, the structure of the wine it produced. But older clones matured too late and virtually none was planted after 1945. Paul Pontallier found new clones allowing the variety to play its rightful role in the blend – another reinforcement for the idea that historically, Margaux was not as capricious, not as "feminine" a wine as was once assumed. Modestly he declares that "the few hectares of Petit Verdot I have planted will be my real memorial".

A crucial tasting for the assemblage. From right to left:
Laura Mentzelopoulos, Paul Pontallier, Jean
Grangerou, Philippe Barré, Professor Emile Peynaud
and Corinne Mentzelopoulos.

Emile Peynaud (above).
The permanent staff at Château Margaux (below).
Following double page: A view of St-Michel from the
château.

THE
VERSAILLES OF THE
MEDOC

In 1810, the Marquis de la Colonilla chose Louis Combes as the architect responsible for creating the new Château Margaux, he did not make his choice lightly. It is possible that he tried to find a Parisian architect, but dissatisfied, fell back on the local school whose talents had been amply proved over the previous half-century in Bordeaux itself. Moreover, Colonilla's elder brother had lived in Bordeaux all his adult life, and Colonilla himself must have known the city well enough by then to know of Combes as the tacitly-acknowledged heir to the great Victor Louis, architect of Bordeaux's famous *Grand Théâtre.*

Combes was the son of a well-known master carpenter, and 20 years younger than Colonilla. He was precociously talented, and a local benefactor paid for his studies in Paris where he won the *Premier Prix* for architecture at the *Ecole des Beaux Arts* before he was 20. Like many younger architects he then spent three years in Rome and travelling around Italy, returning to his native city in the mid- 1780s with his ideas clearly formed.

It was natural for their basis to be classical or neo-classical; his youth after all had been spent in a city where virtually all the most impressive buildings were new and neo-classic. His stay in Italy clearly purified his style, and also provided him with an idea – to be immensely useful when it came to designing Margaux – of how classical buildings should be integrated into the landscape.

Unfortunately for Combes, he found himself unable to exercise his ambitious plans for designing monumental public buildings when he returned home. The private houses (*hôtels*) which he actually built were necessarily limited in size and scope; commissions which called for professional discipline and ingenuity rather than utopian vision. But Combes acquitted himself honourably, and in the Hôtel St-Acquart on the Cours de L'Intendance (now the premises of a famous jeweller) he showed how he could take the received ideas of his time and employ them with a delicacy and dignity all his own. Another commission – for rebuilding Château Olivier at Léognan just south of Bordeaux – was interrupted by the Revolution and never carried through to completion.

As part of an almost apolitical *cultural élite* Combes flourished during Revolutionary times. He revamped a prize-winning design for a cathedral into a suitably grandious home for the National Assembly. He designed a couple of official buildings, now vanished, and acquired a reasonably senior official post. But the majority of his work was still for private clients.

The signature of one of the men who helped to build the château (above).
The peristyle is a perfect expression of the Palladianism associated with Château Margaux. Its simplicity and strong, classical lines dominate the façade of the château (left).

Combes was a strange mixture of the practical architect and the visionary. He put down on paper his ideas and sketches in great profusion – and fortunately a great many of them have been preserved. Besides his uncoordinated notes, Combes also formulated his own aesthetic theories, in lectures and proposed courses on architecture. His ideal was always Greek: he wrote that for him "perfection rests on three basic principles:

unity, simplicity and aptness". He was, above all, backward-looking. Many commentators have remarked on the way Margaux harks back not only to the Greeks, but, more directly, to the neo-classical style prevailing in the Bordeaux of his youth. He strongly disapproved of the liberties he felt were being taken with the purity of the neo-

classical style by more forward-looking architects.

If Combes refused to look forward, he was even more implacably opposed to the medieval fantasies of the Gothic style, its disorder and lack of regularity. This was ironic, for his father's chief claim to fame had been as the carver of the sober Gothic ornaments on the church at Barsac. In the son's search for simplicity and unity he attacks the small scale of Gothic ornamentation. Renaissance architecture was not much better, because although architects tried to imitate the Greek classics, they didn't understand the fundamental rules and were therefore muddled in their thinking. Naturally, he abhorred decorations. In Combes' own words: "At the time of Louis XV architecture degenerated: in decorating buildings they piled on shapes and details of a most unbridled nature. They used ornamentation in the most appalling taste."

One of his more detailed criticisms of Victor Louis' masterpiece, the *Grand Théâtre,* provides a major clue to one of the most important features of Château Margaux, the vastly impressive flight of steps leading up to the base of the columns on the front of the château. The theatre also boasts a much lower and less impressive flight leading up to its peristyle, but this is a nineteenth-century addition. In Combes' time the plinths on which the pillars rested were flush with the pavement. And while Combes admired the peristyle as a whole, in his view it would have produced a much stronger effect if, instead of being built on square plinths, the columns stood directly on a broad staircase with many treads: "the plinths make the base look heavy, and the columns look a little thin: by doing away with the plinths, the columns would gain in stature and would appear broader and much less widely-spaced".

As he confronted the task of designing the château, Combes almost certainly thought back to the last private commission he had undertaken before 1789, which had been interrupted by the Revolution, the enlargement of Château Olivier. In the corner of one of the detailed plans of Olivier there is a tiny drawing of Combes' ideas for adding wings to the existing château. And, as can be seen from one of his first drawings for Margaux (page 39), he reproduced this idea with some fidelity. The basic plan is not too dissimilar from that of an eighteenth-century *chartreuse* in that all

In all of Combes' designs for the interior layout of the
house the main staircase is tucked away to one side.
He finally settled on a sober oval shape (above).
Even at garden level Combes created a warm, spacious
and well-organized interior (right).

the main rooms are on one floor – albeit not on the ground floor but on a mezzanine raised sufficiently to allow for the sweep of the staircase.

Combes' second set of designs shows the outline of the present château in all its glory, massive, solid, with the frontage enlarged sufficiently to provide an adequate framework for the pillars and peristyle. Combes had transformed the second floor under the pillars from mere attics into a proper series of rooms and added a third storey in line with the peristyle – the cornice plays a crucial role in binding the base of the peristyle to the rest of the building.

But even the second version showed some of the faults on which Combes himself had frowned in Victor Louis' *Grand Théâtre*. Both the peristyle and roof were fancy and ornamented. Worse: Combes' friend, the painter Lacour, had designed a triangular decoration for the interior or the peristyle which would have been a masterpiece of bad taste in any epoch, let alone one dedicated to sober purity of style. The design of the roof was more attractively "impure". It was of mansard shape, with dormer windows set into it. Within there was a spiral staircase leading to a small cupola surrounded by a balcony – a charming fantasy but out of keeping with the severity of the overall design, and, of course, alien to the architect's own theories.

The final version – which is the third as far as we know – shows how Combes finally returned to keep faith with his own theories. The peristyle and the cornice are unadorned. Moreover, the roof had been flattened and lowered, and almost all ornament – not to mention little temples and balconies – had been done away with. To the

La cour des artisans.
The principal chai is of massive dimensions and is both
austere and powerful. The oak roof is supported by 18
white stone columns six foot in diameter (left).

119

author's uninstructed eye, this particular result of Combes' drive for purity is a pity: the virtual absence of any feature above the peristyle unbalances the whole. The staircase is bold enough to lead the eye naturally to the columns, but there is no similar substantial feature above the peristyle.

Finally, and the first detail noticed by even the most casual visitor, came the sphinxes, placed squarely at the bottom corners of the stairs, as they were in the first version.

Nearly all the work was done within a year. For we have Combes' drawings of the only decoration he permitted himself marked "ready", dated 29th April 1811, barely a year after the Marquis had originally called on him. These drawings relate to the ceiling above the peristyle – which is invisible until you have actually climbed the stairs. Although one is a mere outline, the other, in Professor Pariset's words, already has its "decorations, rosettes, acanthus leaves, crowns of oak branches united by intertwining links. These design motifs are in the Empire style, and the present sculptures, which faithfully copy them, have been executed to perfection". They prove that "Combes knew how to keep up with the latest fashion".

Within the château the delicate and restrained decorations hinted at on the peristyle become the norm – although they are by no means all in the latest style. For the decorations – chimneys, columns reflecting those of the front, niches for statues, the detailing on doors and cornices – reflect what Professor Pariset calls "a delightful muddle of a number of artistic tendencies".

The interior probably contains roughly the same number of reception and main bedrooms as the château pulled down by Colonilla – three salons, dining and billiard rooms, three master bedrooms, do not constitute a castle Moreover, the house is sensibly arranged. The architect's "indefatigable ingenuity in the search of comfort" has left its marks in the general convenience of the arrangements of servants' and masters' quarters, of rooms and storage space sensibly organized. And the detailing is superb. Professor Pariset sums up the finely wrought decorations throughout the château by declaring that "a logical schematic style triumphs, not at all lacking in imagination, but whimsical and surprising . . . the whole, which is not really Louis XVI and not exactly Empire, is artistically very polished".

Even where there are no decorations – as in the reception hall underneath the *porte-cochère,* the coach entrance under the staircase – the conception is not rigorously square, but imaginatively valuted, arcaded, a lightly airy crypt.

But Combes was not designing a mere château, however impressive. He was super-imposing it on a thriving agricultural business whose buildings were also part of the overall pattern. Whereas the *chais* and the housing for the estate workers around the other châteaux in the village grew up haphazardly, their equivalents at Château Margaux were planned as one, obviously by Combes himself. In designing their layout, he again harked back to his frustrated designs for

A portrait of Alexandre Aguado who bought Château Margaux after the death of Colonilla. He was more interested in refurbishing the interior than the château's architectural qualities.

Château Olivier. There, the working buildings were arranged as wings, detached from, but related to, the château. At Margaux, to the left, is the *cour des artisans,* with the houses and workshops of the innumerable craftsmen required to maintain a largely self-sufficient major estate. There are still a few craftsmen housed in the workshop around the yard and, until a few years ago, there was a much fuller team: a blacksmith, a joiner, a plumber, a mechanic, a mason and a carpenter, each with their assistants, as well as two painters and a roofer to take care of the innumerable buildings in the "village".

Beyond the courtyard is a "village street", a row of 30 or more cottages, although these are too feudally related to the "manor" for the taste of today's estate workers. And just to the left of the main gate, a handsome house for the *maître de chai,* a four-square residence next to the *cuisine des vendanges,* the sort of dower house or bailiff's lodgings found on many estates. The château itself is set back, for the approach leads past the back of the *chais,* which seem from a distance to be detached wings of the château, close enough to remind visitors of the main business of the estate, but not too close to invite familiarity.

It is naturally the principal *chai* which has attracted most of the attention since it was built.

"Just think", wrote Paul de Cassagnac, "of the main wine shed. It is 110 yards long, 25 yards wide and appropriately high. The oak roof is supported by a series of eighteen stone columns six foot in diameter". Indeed the main "first year" *chai* at Margaux could serve as the model for the dozens of other scattered the length and breadth of the Médoc. In principle, such warehouses are simply sheds. They are impressive only because of their dimensions, because of the lack of direct lighting (they have to be well dug-in half underground, well-insulated from the light and air to preclude sudden changes of temperature) and because of the value and reputation of their contents, housed in dozens of new oak casks, all exactly aligned, row upon endless row, all duly stamped with the château's name. M. Pijassou remarks how "many of the *chais* of the best wines of the Médoc seem as vast as a cathedral: that of Château Margaux gives this impression, with its row of white columns (without plinths) with Tuscan capitals".

It was fitting that Margaux's main *chai* should echo – albeit in a simpler, more industrial style – the simplicity and magnificence of the château down to the architect's dislike of plinths. Any lesser accommodation would have been unworthy of the château and of its wine.

Statuette in the reception room of la cour des chais.
Following double page: The wine is decanted before a
meal in order to release the most elegant aromas
associated with Château Margaux.

THE "BEAU IDEAL" OF CLARET

In the first decade of the eighteenth century, when a few named clarets emerged from the ruck, Margaux was one of the four named as outstanding growths. And it has never lost that position. Among its early admirers was the first English Prime Minister, Sir Robert Walpole, and while not the exclusive property of politicians, they were undoubtedly attracted by it. Thomas Jefferson sent a friend ten dozen bottles of the 1784 vintage, "the best vintage which has happened in nine years" he wrote, "and Margaux is one of the four vineyards which are admitted to possess exclusively the first reputation. I may safely assure you therefore, that, according to the taste of this country and of England there cannot be a bottle of better Bordeaux produced in France".

Jefferson went on to note that the wine – at three livres a bottle – was very expensive, but remarked that his friend had not set any price limits. A later President, Nixon, was also keenly aware of the problems posed by the price of wine which provided some solace for him as he cruised, an increasingly beleaguered man, down the Potomac on the Presidential yacht Sequoia during the troubled summer preceding his resignation. "The President had become something of

a wine buff during his New York City days", Woodward and Bernstein tell us in *The Final Days,* "and the Sequoia was stocked with his favourite, a 1966 Château Margaux which sold for about $30 a bottle. He always asked for it when beef was served. And he had issued orders to the stewards about what to do when large groups of Congressmen were aboard. His guests were to be served a rather good $6 wine; his glass was to be filled from a bottle of Château Margaux wrapped in a towel".

More crucial to Margaux's reputation than the tastes of presidents has been the judgement of the marketplace of Bordeaux. Fortunately for the château, the historically crucial test for any claret – the tasting which preceded the submission of a selection of the Gironde's wines for the Universal Exhibition to be held in Paris in 1855 – was a triumph for Margaux. There was never any real question of which wines would be adjudged "first growths" – the order of vinous precedence had been too solidly established by market forces over a century and a half for any sudden change to be made. Nevertheless, the order of precedence within the first growths was a matter of great contention. Lafite, conscious of an historic primacy, was pushing its claims – to exhibit separately, to

At Château Margaux the elegance of the wine is reflected in the table decorations. Creating the right image is very important to the long-term success of the estate.

be awarded a special medal, to be, in fact, not just the *"premier des premiers"*, the "first of the firsts", but in a totally distinct category. The estate's pretensions were finally burst by M. Galos, an official of the Bordeaux Chamber of Commerce, which was organizing the tastings. "I should point out", he noted acidly, "that Château Margaux ought to be placed at the head of its peers because, in the tasting, it obtained 20 marks (presumably out of 20), while Lafite was awarded only 19."

The precedence according in 1855 has assumed an almost mystical significance in Bordeaux since then. But the ultimate test of the wine's quality is not the preference of statesmen, or even of the experts of the Bordeaux wine market, but of

those who know and love wine: and for many of them, as Ian Maxwell Campbell wrote "Margaux is the *beau idéal* of claret". It is normal, and sensible, to place it in the "golden mean" between Lafite and Latour, historically its only equals in the Médoc. Latour the big, implacable, robust wine,

Lafite the most delicate of the three; qualities which each carried the potential corollaries of obvious faults – Latour coarse, Lafite thin. For true Margaux-lovers, then, "their" wine represents an ideal balance between the two extremes.

The judgement is not a new one. In 1815 William Lawton, the wine-broker who then dominated the whole wine market, was probably merely summing up generally received opinion when he wrote in an internal memorandum: "Margaux strikes a nice balance between Lafite and Latour".

During the nineteenth century there was an emerging consensus about the qualities to be associated with the wines produced by the whole commune of Margaux, qualities which naturally found their fullest expression in the wines of the château itself. In the mid-1830s a guidebook to Bordeaux's wines talked of Margaux as "the most delicate and suave of the whole *département*".

But it was Charles Cocks, an English teacher living in Bordeaux, who produced the classic definition of the wines of the château itself, which he called "the most highly regarded of the whole *département*". His description has been quoted, with such regularity over the last 135 years since

A gilded bronze centrepiece decorated with grapes is a fine example of the many works of art that adorn the château. It celebrates the importance of the vine in the history of Margaux.

it first appeared in the mid-1840s in his guide to Bordeaux and its wines that it forms, consciously or not, the foundation for most people's idea of Margaux's qualities. As he wrote "these wines are possessed of much fineness, a beautiful colour, and a very sweet bouquet which perfumes the mouth; they are strong without being intoxicating; invigorate the stomach without affecting the head,

change the nuances of the original. H. Warner Allen for instance, talked of the wine as being "generous without being heady, stimulating the digestion, leaving the hed clear, the breath clean and the mouth fresh". In this (freely acknowledged) adaption Warner Allen makes the wine sound rather like a superior sort of vinous mouthwash.

and leave the breath pure and the mouth cool" – not that his judgement was entirely novel: a similar, though less full description, can be found in the 1833 edition of Cyrus Redding's famous book on wines.

Because Cocks' guidebook was published in both French and English, later writers could

Much later, towards the end of a life devoted to the appreciation of fine wines, Warner Allen came nearest to a generally accepted idea of the – never precisely describable – sensations associated with the appreciation of the finest of wines. He talked of the 1875 vintage as "a lovely wine" possessing "lightness, grace and balance. . .

The dining room, decorated in the Empire style, is a place where wine, rather than food, has the upper hand.

always the hallmarks of Château Margaux". He quotes approvingly another notable wine lover, Morton Shand, who had written of Margaux as "the most delicate and poetic of the three greatest Médocs with one of the most unmistakable flavours in the world and an entrancing cowslip bouquet". "I am not quite sure", Warner Allen commented, "about the cowslip; Château Margaux for me suggests rather the raspberry of the almond. Certainly no wine can equal a fine Margaux in delicate fragrance and subtlety of taste." In the same vein, Charles Walter Berry wrote of the "cedary taste" of Margaux; and everyone who has written about the wine (or even merely savoured it) emphasizes the delicate, flowery bouquet of Margaux, unique among the wines of the Médoc.

The associations – cedar, cowslip, almond, raspberry – are themselves embodiments of the train of thought triggered by the words "delicacy"

"lightness", and above all "elegance" which recur throughout vinous literature whenever Margaux's name is mentioned. But there is an obverse side to the almost magical, ethereal qualities conveyed by these words: a certain fragility which leaves it at the mercy, not only of the elements, so crucial a factor in Bordeaux, but of the need for superior attention to the wine-making as well.

Cocks preceded his eulogy of Margaux's wines with the reservation "in a year favourable to the vine". This is echoed more bluntly by Edmund Penning-Rowsell in his classic *The Wines of Bordeaux,* in which he says that Château Margaux "is noted for its fine bouquet and the delicacy of its flavour". But "on the whole it is a wine particularly successful in fine years, but correspondingly disappointing in off-vintages, although the excellent 1950 is an exception to this". Like so many other authorities he also

Decanting.

makes the point that many of the disappointments encountered with Margaux are due to the human failings of earlier proprietors, but there remains the incontestable fact that, even with the most conscientious of owner and wine-makers, Margaux is a fragile wine.

Hugh Johnson provided an even more brutal summing up a few years ago in his *World Atlas of Wine*. "In great vintages its wine can justify its first growth status: it achieves unique finesse and subtlety. In recent vintages, however, the third growth Palmer has often made better wines." Palmer's vines are, of course, situated opposite Margaux's. The two are, indeed, only a few yards apart at many points. The enigmas posed by the variation in the quality of the wine Margaux produces, as well as some explanation of the unique delights it provides at its finest can however be – albeit partially – provided by the geographers and the geologists.

But Hugh Johnson was referring to the "old", pre-Mentzelopoulos wines, whose qualities, as we saw in Chapter 3 are, supposedly the direct opposite of the vintages since 1977. The principles of selection have indeed, changed dramatically. Paul Pontallier rather gave the game away when he told an interviewer that some wines were difficult to judge "until they have had contact with the oak. If the oak dominates the wine it means that the wine lacks the power and structure we are looking for".

As we saw William Lawton noted the same qualities nearly two centuries ago. But at some point after that a tradition grew up, of the softer more "feminine" wines described above. In the intervening period the power over the taste of the wine, even of the First Growths, passed to the merchants on the Quai des Chartrons who bought the wines early, sometimes "*sur souches*" before the grapes were ripe, whisked the new wine straight from the fermenting vat and matured it in their cellars: and they, in turn, were dominated by the supposed (and actual) tastes of the British aristocracy. Since the late seventeenth century they had wanted claret to resemble port rather than "clairet", the thin youthful plonk which had first made the name of Bordeaux famous in the Middle Ages.

The merchants' trickery cannot be sufficiently emphasized. Moreover, their knaveries lasted at least until World War II. Professor Peynaud started work at Calvet, then the most important firm in Bordeaux, in 1937, and during his time there, which lasted over a decade, he reckons that not a single bottle left the cellars without the addition of at least 15 per cent of stronger wine, mostly from Algeria and the Rhône.

At first glance this sustained mass trickery, practised for nearly 200 years, seems totally incompatible with the manifest, and manifestly enormous, perceived differences in the wines from the châteaux with which the Milords were familiar. But these were extremely limited in number. Remember they were largely unfamiliar with the wines of St-Emilion (apart from Cheval Blanc), the châteaux of Pomerol, even Petrus, were a curiosity, and their acquaintance even with the wines of the Médoc was almost entirely confined to a handful of classed growths.

So each major merchant produced his own version of each of the major growths – this is no joke, old Bordeaux hands remember one of the Harvey family keeping a mouthful of Pontet-Canet unswallowed until he arrived at the next port of call, the better to compare the versions of the château's wines produced by the two firms. And clearly the winner would be, not only the firm which produced the best version, but also the one which corresponded most closely to the customers' perceived image of the château's wines. So, once a château had acquired a reputation for producing "feminine" wines, liable to be unreliable in poor years, it was stuck with the image.

Claude Bizard is responsible for the decanting and service of the wines at Château Margaux.

Clearly there had to be a basis for the opinion, an Ur-Margaux, as it were, but this could easily have resulted from the very different viticultural techniques employed at each château, and the very marked difference in the wines before they were stiffened by their "*Travail à l'Anglaise*" on the Quai des Chartrons. The obvious case is Latour. In the 1930s the château was an enthusiastic chaptalizer: and local folk-memory has it that bags of plaster were dumped in each vat to absorb excess water and thus strengthen and thicken the wine.

Yet the capacity of Margaux's *terroir* to produce sturdy wines, the association of Margaux with "power and structure", was not lost, rather buried beneath the legend and the reputation, in the century and a half between Lawton's comments and the arrival of the André Mentzelopoulos. The "underlying" Margaux did surface at times during the most complete survey of the estate ever conducted, a massive tasting of 70 vintages of the château's wines organized by the Californian millionaire Bipin Desai, in May 1987.

Such massive "vertical" tastings produce endless comparisons, which can be extremely dangerous because it is often difficult to know the provenance of the wines. Any wine that left the château unbottled was almost certainly tampered with on a massive scale. The only pure wine on the market came from the château itself. This was often the best the estate could produce, parallel to the few casks retained for the delectation of the Marquis d'Aulede in the late seventeenth century, wine made exclusively from the Cap de Haut and the Puch sem Peyre.

But in modern "vertical" tastings one is never quite sure of the provenance of the wine. If it comes from the château, its character is liable to be very different from wine of the same vintage which had been worked in Bordeaux.

But the balance between "château" and "merchant's" wines varied wildly. For long periods – notably for the half-century following the collapse of the market and the arrival of the mildew at the end of the 1870s – the merchants were in total control, whereas for a short period during the 1860s and 1870s some châteaux (notably, as we saw, Margaux) had absentee owners only really interested in the prestige attached to ownership of the estate. They would allow their wines to be "abonnés", sub-contracted for decades at a stretch, to a handful of leading merchants.

Château-bottling may have been a proof of purity, but was emphatically not a guarantee of consistency. The art of *assemblage* was in its infancy – as we saw, when the Ginestets took over they found that all the wine was, effectively, being poured into one vat. Bottling was a casual affair, carried out in the estate workers' spare time over a period of six months or more, including heatwaves and cold spells, conditions certain to affect the quality of the wine.

At these tastings even the millionaire beggars cannot be choosers. In only a few instances (most obviously at Mouton and Lafite, in Rothschild hands for over a century) are there enough wines available whose whole life has been passed under controlled conditions at the château itself – so not

The cork, hung at the neck of the decanter, allows the vintage to be identified (above). The wine is often decanted even for an informal meal (left).

surprisingly it is far easier in these cases to assemble more reliable proof of the châteaux' past greatness. In most other cases including, and especially, Margaux, where the Mentzelopoulos' had to buy in stocks of even relatively recent vintages like the 1966, the bottles had been matured and then stored under very different conditions, so, inevitably no taster expected two bottles from the same vintage to taste alike.

Nevertheless there remains a division. Vintages where château bottling (however rough and ready) predominated will be truer to the original than vintages dominated by "merchant's" wines. Having said all that, and however many hedges surround the results of these tastings, they are bound to be fascinating – and to anyone, like myself, who believes that the *terroir* underlies the basic style of any wine, they are bound to have a certain validity. This does not mean that they will be consistent. After the tasting Desai is reported* as saying that the wines divided into several distinct catergories. One fits the classic image of the château. They were "opulent, velvety, seductive, intensely charming, superbly balanced and so on. These would have seemed ready to drink early and will remain drinkable almost forever. They were, for example 1982, 1953 and 1900".

Now compare the opinions of Desai, still,

"Pavillon Blanc", made entirely from Sauvignon Blanc, is a fresh but fittingly elegant dry white. It was first marketed during World War II.

* In *Decanter,* November 1987, the source of all the quotations.

despite his experience, a relatively "amateur" taster, with those of Michael Broadbent, the possessor of the world's finest palate for old wines, a palate honed over a quarter of a century of regularly tasting rare vintages. He was less dogmatic than Desai, finding the 1982 "fleshy, spicy, lovely fruit, lots of tannin masked by beguiling softness".

But two of Desai's other categories fit far less well into the classic Margaux mould. One came from famously hot vintages, like 1893 and 1947 (to which will have to be added 1989 in due course). They were "almost Burgundy-like, intense, high in alcohol." Without being overly cynical, the "Burgundian" character could have resulted, like that of the wines of Beaune in the past, from the inclusion of a generous dose of wine from the Rhône. Broadbent found the 1893 "full, rich, very positive but with an acid edge" – his equivalent of Desai's "Burgundy". The best of the two bottles of the 1947 had "perfect bouquet and flavour.... Slightly sweet, rich, great length".

Desai had another category: "tannic, hugely concentrated with deep colour", wines from classic vintages when Margaux was, supposedly, producing delicate wines: 1961, 1945, 1928, 1870 and 1865.

In all this confusion our best idea of the underlying historic taste of the château comes, not from Desai's superficially contradictory but perfectly valid impressions, but from the opportunity provided by the tasting to sample a run of wines from a period when the château enjoyed stable and careful management under the Ginestets.

The improvements started as soon as Fernand took over in 1933. But the improvement accelerat-

ed after 1950 when the Ginestets finally stopped allowing anyone else to bottle their wine. Not surprisingly the last "Ginestet" vintage truly worthy of the château came in 1966. By that time Margaux had lost its way, and Pierre Ginestet had embarked on his ill-fated experiment in marketing "non-millésime" wines, from which the château did not recover until he sold the estate.

The glories of the first two decades of "Ginestet" Margaux were confirmed by Michael Broadbent, who "observed that the somewhat maligned Ginestet's had made, with the aid of good weather, some outstandingly delectable wines. The top vintages of Margaux from 1950 to 1966 could scarcely be faulted".

But the improvement had started earlier, with the only two half-decent vintages of that miserable decade, the 1930s. The two bottles of the 1934 vintage showed, not only the many various qualities of "Margaux Ginestet-style", but also the very different qualities perceptible even in two bottles of such a relatively recent vintage ("Note how levels and condition can vary", wrote Michael Broadbent of the two bottles of the 1945 at the tasting".). One bottle of the 1934 had a "surprisingly deep intense and impressive appearance; chocolaty, a certain opulence (like 1934 Latour), nice but stalky. Sweet on palate, rich, soft underbelly, a bit edgy". The other bottle, from Calvet, was not merely "edgy", it was "living dangerously", although the bouquet had "more charm and fruit" and the wine was "rich, flavoury".

The 1937 turned out to be what the Bordelais call a *fausse bonne année*" a vintage which did

*The label design has not been changed since the
beginning of the century.*

not live up to its early promise. "Not my favourite vintage" declares Broadbent, but "Margaux about the best". Of the wines at the tasting, one had "bouquet of clean old cedar crossed with gently gnarled oak... dryish, fullish, chewy, still with 1937 tannin and acidity". The other had a "bouquet of vanilla and ivy. Edgy on palate".

Of the two 1945s, one had "deep colour, deep, rich, perfect bouquet. Excellent length". The other was "less deep, more evolved; charming, creamy bouquet, held well; dry, fullish firm, fine – still years of life. A great vintage, great wine". One of the bottles of the 1947 had a "perfect bouquet and flavour. Slightly sweet, rich, great length". The nose of the other bottle "fairly belched out the heat of the vintage, of singed grapes, slightly malted and clearly a bit oxidised. Thickness and weight reminded me of 1947 Cheval Blanc". The heat of the 1949 had a different effect. One of the bottles "was distinctly sweet on the palate, fullish, rather hot Graves-like flavour", while the other bottle of the same vintage was "fragrant, biscuity, perfect".

In 1950 Margaux broke all the rules. In a generally mediocre year it yet produced undeniably the best wine of the vintage, with "a gentle fragrance; slightly sweet, medium weight, lovely flavour, tannin and acidity holding it together well, excellent aftertaste". The 1953 showed fully the qualities of that magic year: "Medium, tile red; and exciting whiff of seaweed and iodine, blossoming into a glorious classic claret scent – with flavour to match. Great length, perfect balance, still refreshing". The 1952 had "an immediate lovely rich biscuity bouquet," but it was "lacking the lush feminity and opulence of the 1953".

The 1955 was classic "old-style" Margaux with

In the château's ancient kitchen a simple meal is laid out, and in the time-honoured tradition, it is accompanied by Château Margaux.

its "fresh mushroom skin, then a gentle whole-meal biscuit fragrance... fading gracefully. A perfectly delightful beverage now". By contrast the 1959 was a "lovely tile red with heart of ruby; harmonious bouquet, with great vinosity, warm brick, hot-vintage singed, creamy vanillin, blossoming into a glorious biscuity/liquorice scent; on the palate sweet, fullish, lovely, flavoury, certainly no shortage of acidity".

Naturally enough the Ginestet era reached its apogee in 1961 which had a "glorious ripe mulberry bouquet. It seemed to waft out of the glass in endless changing waves, with a lovely sweet fresh-picked mushrooms scent after 30 minutes. Distinctly sweet on entry, mouth-filling body, flavour, extract. Concentrated yet full of charm. Fleshy. Great length. Great wine".

But the glory days were not over, as shown by the last three decent vintages of the classic Ginestet years. The 1962 had a "fragrant bouquet with Margaux's violet scent... dryish, lean, elegant, still tannin and acidity. It would be nice if the 1981 turned out like this". The start of the decline was noticeable in the 1964 which had a "fragrant, slightly peppery bouquet; hint of tobacco; medium, positive mid-flavour but somewhat hard and lacking the rich chunkiness of the best 1964s". But there was still a great wine to come, the 1966, which was "still deep-coloured; fragrant, oyster-shells – a whiff of sea breeze, developed beautifully, sweet, elegant, ripe; lovely shape and texture in the mouth, flesh, length. A great wine with years in hand". To which one can only add, thank you *terroir,* thank you Ginestets – and all the other owners, from the D'Aulèdes to the Mentzelopoulos, who have lavished their care and capital on these very special slopes.

"There cannot be a better bottle of Bordeaux produced in France." So wrote Thomas Jefferson on sending a friend ten bottles of Château Margaux 1784.

Following page: Menus celebrating the visits of Leonid Brezhnev in October 1971 and Her Majesty Queen Elizabeth II in May 1972.

DINER

en l'honneur de

SON EXCELLENCE

MONSIEUR LÉONIDE I. BREJNEV

SECRÉTAIRE GÉNÉRAL DU COMITÉ CENTRAL
DU PARTI COMMUNISTE DE L'UNION SOVIÉTIQUE
MEMBRE DU PRAESIDIUM DU SOVIET SUPRÊME DE L'U.R.S.S.

et de

MADAME BREJNEV

Palais du Grand Trianon
Lundi 25 Octobre 1971

Foie gras du Quercy

Suprêmes de turbot Joinville

Selle d'agneau Armenonville

Cœurs de laitues

Fromages

Soufflé glacé au Grand Marnier

Château Suduiraut 1967
Meursault-Charmes 1969
Château Margaux 1962

Dom Pérignon 1964

DINER

en l'honneur de

SA MAJESTÉ

LA REINE ELIZABETH II

et de

SON ALTESSE ROYALE
LE PRINCE PHILIP, DUC D'EDIMBOURG

Palais du Grand Trianon
Lundi 15 mai 1972

Parfait de foie gras du Perigord

Croustade de langoustes Gastronome

Baron de Pauillac Saint-Florentin

Haricots verts Maître d'Hôtel

Cœurs de laitues

Fromages

Nougatine glacée aux framboises

Château d'Yquem 1949
Corton Charlemagne 1964
Château Margaux 1959
Dom Pérignon 1962

APPENDIXES

VINTAGE NOTES

All the vintages since 1945 have been listed in these tables. For those before 1945, only the very good ones, and the ones still of interest today, are included. The information has been compiled from documents kept at the château since 1795 when Mathieu Miqueau handed the estate over. For the vintages after 1918, they are based on the château's cellarbook. The star ratings, ranging from ***** (outstanding) to – (poor), are based on Michael Broadbent's assessment of the vintages in *The Great Vintage Wine Book II* (1991). The ratings generally refer to the quality and condition of the wine when last tasted. The comments were made by the *maître de chai* in November 1988 and updated in 1990.

VINTAGE	CONDITIONS	COMMENTS	CASES PRODUCED	VINTAGE ASSESSMENT
1989	The whole year – like 1983 – was particularly hot and dry, so that the grapes reached an exceptional level of maturity and concentration very early; this was the earliest harvest in the century, beginning 9 September.	This vintage is a very harmonious blend of the strength and the elegance of the greatest Margaux wines. The nose is classic, rich and complex; the first impression in the mouth is surprisingly round, soft and sweet, then powerful, dense and very long. A truly great vintage.	21,800	*****
1988	The beginning of the season was rather difficult with June and early July particularly rainy, but after 10 July it was very hot and dry until the end of the harvest, so that, once again, the grapes could reach an excellent level of maturity. (The *vendange* began 3 October).	A typical vintage of Château Margaux, very fine and elegant, together with a lot of concentration and depth.	21,500	*****
1987	August and September were very good months (September was particularly hot and dry), which allowed the grapes to achieve a high level of ripeness. Sadly, at the time of the *vendange* it started to rain, spoiling the high hopes for this vintage. (The *vendange* began 5 October.)	It is under difficult conditions such as these that a truly great *terroir* reveals itself. Château Margaux 1987 is a particularly powerful wine for the year, marked, equally, by a great finesse and an aromatic complexity.	13,700	***
1986	A superb vintage, characterized by a hot, dry summer, (serious drought in July and August). After a short rainy spell in September, good weather returned until the end of the *vendange*. Once again the grapes achieved a high level of ripeness in a perfectly healthy state. (The *vendange* began 27 September.)	Another exceptional wine, but different to the preceding one; characterized by an extraordinary richness and tannic concentration. You would have to go back to the legendary 1961 to find such a powerful wine.	25,400	*****
1985	After a normal spring and summer, the months of September and October were exceptionally hot and dry, giving the grapes an excellent level of ripeness. Perfectly healthy crop. (The *vendange* began 26 September.)	Exceptional, particularly fine, rich and elegant. On the palate, one is struck immediately by the delicacy and charm of its round, velvety, almost silky, tannic taste. The length and concentration also confirm that this is an excellent vintage.	25,000	*****
1984	Cold and rainy weather during flowering (June) caused widespread *coulure* for the Merlot and the Cabernet Franc. The summer was warm and sunny, but heavy rains in September hampered the ripening process. Picking was held back and, luckily, there was another sunny period, which meant that the grapes achieved sufficient ripeness in what proved to be a difficult year. (The *vendange* began 1 October.)	Remarkable vintage for the year. A very clear, fine and fruity nose. Powerful and slightly austere to the taste.	15,500	***
1983	Once again a splendid, hot, late season. The sunny and dry conditions caused a remarkable maturity in an abundant vintage. (The *vendange* began 29 September.)	A classic Margaux, characterized by a remarkably complex, rich and elegant nose. On the palate there is a strong tannic taste, but well-matured and without astringency or harshness. A truly exceptional wine.	29,200	*****
1982	It is very rare that these conditions are found together: April, hot and dry; June, slightly stormy; the summer months, very hot, especially the first two weeks of September – a combina-	Vintage unparalleled for its quality and quantity. The exceptional ripeness of the grape gave the wine concentration with a	29,300	*****

VINTAGE	CONDITIONS	COMMENTS	CASES PRODUCED	VINTAGE ASSESSMENT
	tion which encouraged the grape to ripen remarkably. Excellent weather up to picking. (The *vendange* began 20 September.)	lot of tannin, yet at the same time, staying gentle. A complex, rich and fruity aroma.		
1981	A disastrous spring. A hot and dry August. A satisfactory September with a few days of rain before the harvest, then exceptional weather during the picking. (The *vendange* began 1 October.)	A very fine wine of distinction and elegance. A beautiful tannic structure.	20,000	****
1980	Cold and rainy weather during the spring and early summer delayed the growth of the vine and restricted the flowering. Hot and sunny in September and a little rain in October. Unlike its neighbours, Margaux waited longer before beginning to harvest, with the result that the grapes were perfectly mature. (The *vendange* began 17 October.)	A great wine for the year, ripe and concentrated, with beautiful body. Serious and full-bodied, with a scented aroma.	16,200	**
1979	Rainy spring, dry July, cold August. Good weather in September and October (hot and dry) resulted in a voluminous, healthy and mature crop. (The *vendange* began 4 October.)	Very deep colour, complex aroma of ripe fruit. Moderately tannic, exceptional concentration, great persistence.	17,400	****
1978	A damp, cold spring slowed down the growth of the vines. A beautiful summer, but not enough to make up for lost time. A long and very hot period in September and October encouraged the grapes to ripen well. (The *vendange* began 9 October.)	Deep purple colour, intense and fruity nose, peppery finish. A deep, supple, full bodied wine with a long life. Remarkable.	15,300	****
1977	A heavy frost at Easter (with snow in Bordeaux) reduced the crop's potential. Rather a cold year with a lot of rain in June, July and August. Dry weather in September and harvesting in good conditions. (The *vendange* began 10 October.)	Excellent colour and good body for the year. A strict selection process made this one of the best wines of 1977.	10,100	*
1976	The hottest year for 27 years. Very dry in April, June, July and August. Rain in September diluted a crop that, thus far, held promise. (The *vendange* began 13 September.)	Very nice bouquet. Full and supple wine that ought to develop quickly.	20,000	***
1975	Very hot June and July. September was variable: a little rain just before picking, but during the *vendange* it was hot and sunny. (The *vendange* began 25 September.)	Firm and tannic wine: rich and powerful.	15,300	****
1974	Normal summer, quite hot, but September was cold and rainy. (The *vendange* began 20 September.)	Light and short wine.	14,000	***
1973	Characterized by a very hot August, the hottest since 1949. But September was cold and very rainy. (The *vendange* began 26 September.)	A fine but quite light wine.	15,600	***
1972	Particularly cold and slow year. Despite good, dry weather for the harvest, all the 1972s were affected by the lack of sun. (The *vendange* began 10 October.)	Light wine characterized by its lack of maturity.	19,000	**
1971	Very bad weather at the time of flowering caused significant *coulure* and reduced the potential crop. Very hot weather in July and August, but rain in September. (The *vendange* began 28 September.)	Very fine and elegant nose; less body than the 1970. Good, full structure.	16,000	***
1970	An exceptional year. A very dry summer and an excellent September. Superb conditions for the *vendange*. (The *vendange* began 26 September.)	The most abundant crop for many years, with a quality all the more striking after the 1968 and 1969. Complex bouquet, rich and firm constitution.	25,200	****
1969	After a hot, dry summer, hopes were dashed during an extremely wet September. (The *vendange* began 29 September.)	Fine, light wine, marked by dilution of grapes by rain in September.	10,000	**
1968	Late year; after a normal start to the season, August and September were very rainy. (The *vendange* began 30 September.)	Created under very difficult conditions, the 1968 Margaux is a rapidly maturing, light wine.	8,000	–

VINTAGE	CONDITIONS	COMMENTS	CASES PRODUCED	VINTAGE ASSESSMENT
1967	Erratic, dry year. (The *vendange* began 27 September.)	Fine, pleasant bouquet; supple, full-bodied wine, but a little light.	21,000	**
1966	After a rainy July, a hot August and a sunny September, grapes were harvested under perfect conditions. (The *vendange* began 20 September.)	Rich, fruity and elegant nose and taste. Well-structured. A full wine.	19,000	****
1965	After a warm summer, the month of September was catastrophically rainy, resulting in a lightning deterioration of the grapes. (The *vendange* began 1 October.)	No Château Margaux produced.	0	–
1964	June and July were hot and dry. September was very hot. Rain in the last six days of picking. The first batch – the most important – was very mature, concentrated and healthy; the second batch; harvested in the rain, did not have the same quality. (The *vendange* began 21 September.)	Delicate perfume. Full, harmonious and supple wine.	16,000	***
1963	A bad year: cold and rainy. (The *vendange* began 26 September.)	Rather mediocre wine.	15,000	–
1962	Late picking in good conditions. (The *vendange* began 3 October.)	A seductive wine, eclipsed by 1961.	14,000	***
1961	There was a heavy frost at the end of March, when growth was already underway, followed by a substantial *coulure*, provoked by a short but intense cold spell at the end of May. The potential crop was dramatically reduced. A hot summer but, above all, a very dry September (one of the driest ever known) produced a crop of exceptional maturity and concentration. (The *vendange* began 19 September.)	Intense depth of colour. Very mellow and concentrated bouquet and taste from a perfectly ripened grape. Rich, deep and long-lasting.	8,200	*****
1960	A very early year from the onset (half in flower at the end of May). But the summer was cold and rainy, and September equally rainy. (The *vendange* began 13 September.)	A light but fine and elegant wine; quick maturing.	15,000	**
1959	A lot of rain before the harvest and hot weather during the harvest, made vinification difficult (problems cooling down the must). Very ripe and healthy grapes. (The *vendange* began 24 September.)	Proclaimed the "vintage of the century" before the *vendange*. Great concentration and power, with a lot of roundness and complexity.	19,000	*****
1958	After a very rainy August, September turned out to be good and hot. On the whole, the harvesting conditions were satisfactory. (The *vendange* began 6 October.)	Fine wine, but lacking in body.	10,000	**
1957	Several frosts in April and May. Very cool weather until picking began. A record hot October salvaged this late harvest. (The *vendange* began 4 October.)	A firm wine, but a little hard when it was young. Nevertheless, it is a good and elegant wine.	11,000	*
1956	In spite of a harsh winter (-20°C [-4°F] in Bordeaux, with heavy snowfalls) the vines suffered little at Margaux, but the vegetation developed very late and the cold rainy summer sealed the sad fate of this vintage. (The *vendange* began 8 October.)	Light, round wines, not lacking in finesse, but in body.	8,700	–
1955	A little rain in July; August, hot and dry; no rain at all during September. Ideal harvesting conditions. (The *vendange* began 22 September.)	A lot of charm and finesse. Well balanced.	20,000	***
1954	Very cold and rainy; one of the coldest years since the start of the century. (The *vendange* began 12 October.)	A rather mediocre wine, but still characterized by the finesse of the *terroir*.	6,000	*
1953	This vintage was "made" in August, a really exceptional month, with a little rain and a lot of hot weather. The weather was a little more unstable in September, but conditions were very favourable at the time of the *vendange*. A perfectly healthy crop. (The *vendange* began 26 September.)	A superb wine, one of the best 1953s.	16,000	*****

VINTAGE	CONDITIONS	COMMENTS	CASES PRODUCED	VINTAGE ASSESSMENT
1952	Everything seemed to indicate an exceptional vintage: a very hot June, July and August. But, as is so often the case in Bordeaux, it was a cold and rainy September which determined the outcome, with three weeks of continuous rain. (The *vendange* began 15 September.)	A silky, round, harmonious wine.	13,000	***
1951	Cold and rainy year. (The *vendange* began 1 October.)	A light, fairly fine wine, but lacking in character and body.	11,000	–
1950	A little rain in September but, in general, good weather throughout the year. (The *vendange* began 18 September.)	A very charming and elegant wine, considered to be one of the best of 1950.	18,000	**
1949	A dry but, above all, an extremely hot year. In July and August the heat and the drought caused serious fires in the forests of the Landes. (The *vendange* began 28 September.)	A very concentrated, rich and powerful wine, more well-built than the 1947.	8,500	*****
1948	Average year, very much standard but, unfortunately, falling between two excellent vintages. (The *vendange* began 23 September.)	Concentrated, powerful and fairly tannic wine.	10,000	***
1947	Along with 1945, 1946 and 1949 this was one of the hottest years of the century. Forty-two days of tropical heat, throughout the summer. (The *vendange* began 16 September.)	Very pretty, elegant and complex bouquet. Fine, charming wine.	11,000	****
1946	Average year, but bad maturing conditions. (The *vendange* began 1 October.)	A rather mediocre wine.	6,500	–
1945	Early development of the vines. Dramatic frost on 2 May, with snow in Bordeaux. A very hot and dry summer made the grapes extremely concentrated. (The *vendange* began 12 September.)	A tiny crop for the year of Victory. Powerful, complex, strong tannic richness, ample and fleshy. A fabulous vintage.	7,500	*****
1943	A hot year with hardly any rain. an early vegetal cycle, with flowering complete as early as the end of May. (The *vendange* began 16 September.)	Despite difficulties caused by the war, this was fairly successful vintage: a delicate and elegant wine.	7,500	***
1937	Very little rain throughout the year, apart from just before harvesting. Picking took place in perfect weather. (The *vendange* began 21 September.)	After the 1934, this was one of the best vintages of the 1930s. Rich and savoury, but lighter than the 1934.	8,000	**
1934	Beautiful, dry summer followed by good harvesting conditions. (The *vendange* began 14 September.)	The biggest and the best crop of the 1930s. Rich and full wine with a lot of tannin; a little hard.	18,000	***
1929	Hot and extremely dry year (the driest since the start of the century). A little rain just before the harvest followed by good weather. (The *vendange* began 26 September.)	Big crop. Very elegant wine, less powerful than the 1928.	16,000	*****
1928	Marvellous weather from flowering up until picking, spoiled by a little rain in August. (The *vendange* began 25 September.)	An abundant harvest. Strong, rich and concentrated. An extraordinary vintage, considered today to be superior to the 1929.	16,500	*****
1926	Hot summer without any rain. Late *vendange* in sunny conditions. (The *vendange* began 4 October.)	Small crop due to a poor flowering. Very good wine, powerful and rich, moderately tannic at the finish.	6,000	****
1924	A lot of rain in August, then more variable weather in the harvest period. (The *vendange* began 19 September.)	First year of compulsory château bottling; a turning-point. . . . An abundant crop. A charming and well-structured wine.	19,000	***
1923	Uncertain weather throughout the year. (The *vendange* began 1 October.)	Perfumed nose, but a little light on the palate.	9,500	**
1921	Exceptional heat during the picking. Difficult vinification. (The *vendange* began 15 September.)	Small crop. Elegant and well-structured wine.	8,000	***
1920	Very good September, despite a little rain. (The *vendange* began 22 September.)	Average crop. Elegant and supple wine.	11,000	****

VINTAGE	CONDITIONS	COMMENTS	CASES PRODUCED	VINTAGE ASSESSMENT
1918	Perfect weather for the duration of the harvest. A beautiful and healthy crop. (The *vendange* began 19 September.)	Average crop. A powerful wine, but a little hard and rugged.	11,500	***
1917	Unstable summer, but the *vendange* took place under perfect conditions. (The *vendange* began 22 September.)	Small crop. Not a very rich wine.	8,800	**
1911	A terribly hot summer. The fine weather lasted until the end of the harvest. (The *vendange* began 8 September.)	Small crop. A good 1911.	7,500	**
1909	Good weather, in general, throughout the *vendanges*. (The *vendange* began 29 September.)	A light wine in a fairly difficult year.	9,500	*
1908	Very warm weather throughout the *vendange*, with the exception of three days of rain. (The *vendange* began 21 September.)	The year of the creation of Pavillon Rouge. A small yield due to the frosts between 21 and 26 April, and a severe viral attack called *"Eudemis"*.	9,000	**
1907	It started to rain on 27 September and kept raining but the crop was completely healthy. (The *vendange* began 26 September.)	Charming, elegant and supple wine.	14,500	**
1905	Rain during the *vendange*, except on the first two and the last two days. Healthy crop, despite the rain. (The *vendange* began 21 September.)	Not a very powerful wine, but fine and delicate.	16,000	***
1900	A very hot summer, and severe heat during the *vendange*. Very ripe grapes. (The *vendange* began 24 September.)	An abundant crop and extraordinary wine for the start of the century.	29,000	*****
1899	Difficult, dry summer, but an excellent crop. (The *vendange* began 21 September.)	Crop reduced by the drought. Very mature, excellent quality.	19,000	****
1898	Hot and sunny weather up to the end of September, then rain. (The *vendange* began 24 September.)	Small crop, due to the humidity. Wine, a little hard and tannic.	13,500	**
1896	Variable weather at the start of the *vendange*. Very mature grapes. (The *vendange* began 19 September.)	Immense harvest. Fine and elegant wine.	37,000	****
1893	A vintage that was considered at the time to have benefited from the most extraordinary weather for two centuries. The heat-wave started on 1 March and went on throughout the summer. The whole growing cycle started early; flowering, *veraison* (the moment when the grape begins to ripen and to change colour) and consequently harvesting, began earlier than ever before. An indispensable reprieve after the difficult years caused by disease, parasites and disastrous weather conditions. (The *vendange* began 17 August.)	Legendary, record harvest. An astonishing year, allying superb quality and quantity. Picking had to be stopped for ten days due to lack of vats.	36,000	****
1892	Ideal weather and healthy crop. (The *vendange* began 19 September.)	Good wine but a little light.	18,500	*
1887	Hot summer and a sunny *vendange*. Mildew had been a serious problem in the 1880s, until 1886. The cellar-book at Margaux notes that the fungus was at last under control, thanks to crop spraying with *bouillie bordelaise*. Almost at the same time, Bordeaux fell victim to another plague – the most well known, in fact – phylloxera (a tiny aphid which attacks the roots of the vine). The phylloxera plague started around 1877 and only eventually came to an end when virtually all the vines were replaced by vinestocks grafted onto American rootstock resistant to phylloxera. (The *vendange* began 22 September.)	A small crop; rich wine.	11,000	**
1870	Along with 1864, the best vintage before phylloxera. Only one day of rain during the *vendange*. (The *vendange* began 10 September.)	A remarkable wine.	16,500	*****

VINTAGE	CONDITIONS	COMMENTS	CASES PRODUCED	VINTAGE ASSESSMENT
1868	Overwhelming heat lasting for nine days. (The *vendange* began 7 September.)	Tannic wine without much finesse.	14,000	**
1865	Brilliant sunshine; very early harvesting and very ripe grapes. (The *vendange* began 5 September.)	Very abundant crop. Good wine, but very tannic, which required a long time to mature.	20,000	*****
1864	Despite seven days of rain during the harvest, this was truly a "great" vintage in the golden age of Bordeaux (1858-1878). Previously, oidium had devastated the vineyard from 1854-1857. In 1857 it was successfully eliminated thanks to simple spraying, with sulphur. Significant replanting then followed, causing the leap in production. In the 1860s, production at Margaux was 50 per cent greater than it had been before the oidium. (The *vendange* began 17 September.)	Very good wine, powerful and complex; fabulous bouquet.	15,000	*****
1848	Marvellous weather with no rain. (The *vendange* began 21 September.)	Big harvest; very good wine, powerful and enriched.	12,000	–
1847	Magnificent weather, very hot and dry. (The *vendange* began 25 September.)	Significant harvest. A lot of finesse, but the wine lacked a little body.	14,000	–
1791	"Considered the best that France has produced for many years, and similar is difficult at this time to be obtained, and now in order for bottling". Extract from a wine sales catalogue at Christie's, 23 May 1797. (1)			
1771	The first Bordeaux vintage to appear in a Christie's catalogue, in March 1776. "Excellent fine flavoured Claret of the year 1771".			

(1) Source: Michael Broadbent *The Great Vintage Wine Book.*

MARGAUX PRICES AT AUCTION

This table clearly indicates the very wide range of vintages of Margaux which appeared at auction over the past few seasons. All were sold at Christie's in London and prices are expressed in £s per case unless otherwise indicated (see abbreviations below). The highest price obtained for each vintage is shown.

Abbreviations: B = per bottle M = per magnum 6M = per 6 magnums D = double magnum.

Mid, low and upper refer to the level of wine in the bottle, With older vintages, corks over 20 years begin to lose their elasticity and levels can change. Mid is mid-shoulder, low is low-shoulder and upper is upper-shoulder.

VINTAGE	PRICE	YEAR OF SALE	VINTAGE	PRICE	YEAR OF SALE
1848	880 B	1986		750	1988
1868	500 B	1986		2,600 (upper)	1990
1869	330 B	1986		220 B	1990
1877	115 B	1981	1929	1,600	1988
1887	210 B	1988		220 B	1990
1890	115 B (low)	1990		1,500	1990
1891	340 B	1986	1934	100 B	1988
1892	340 B	1986		1,050	1989
1893	520 B	1986	1937	500	1985
1894	240 B	1989	1940	350 24H	1988
1896	175 B	1986		20 H	1990
1898	220 B	1986	1941	60 B	1986
1899	460 B	1986	1945	140 B	1988
1900	720 B	1986		3,100	1989
1905	185 B	1986		3,300 6M	1989
1907	150 B	1986		290B	1990
1908	116 B	1986	1947	1,000	1988
1909	153 B	1986		40 H	1989
1911	87 B	1985		250 M	1990
1914	100 B (mid)	1988		650 UK	1990
1915	60 B	1989		54 B	1990
(belived to be)			1948	240 M	1988
1916	420	1984	1949	1,450	1988
1917	155 B	1986		2,100 6M	1988
1918	150 B	1986		140 M	1989
1920	153 B	1987	1950	105 M	1987
	110 B	1989		610	1988
1921	83 M	1985	1951	440	1986
1923	50 B	1988	1952	65 M	1989
	170 M	1988	1953	125 M	1988
	460	1989		1,350	1988
1924	230 M	1987		360 M	1990
	160 M	1990	1955	125 M	1988
1925	155 M	1987		600	1988
	750	1987		720	1989
1926	170 B	1987		55 B	1989
	210 M	1987		680 6M	1989
	82 B	1988	1956	185	1988
1928	193 B	1988		115 24H	1988

VINTAGE	PRICE	YEAR OF SALE
1957	400	1990
	260	1988
	320	1989
	370	1990
1958	190	1986
	300	1990
1959	70 B	1988
	850	1988
	1,300	1990
	95 B	1990
1960	190	1988
	130 24H	1988
1961	1,850	1988
	3,100	1990
	160 B	1990
	460 M	1990
	850 DM	1990
1962	40 B	1988
	420	1988
	600	1990
	540 6M	1990
	75 M	1990
1964	300 6M	1988
	350 M	1988
	520	1990
1966	620 6M	1988
	720 M	1988
	370 UK	1989
	650 24H	1989
	750	1990
	600 6M	1990
	65 B	1990
1967	260	1987
	310	1990
	260 6M	1990
1968	125	1985
1969	240	1988
	250	1989
	160 24H	1989

VINTAGE	PRICE	YEAR OF SALE
1970	170	1990
	390 6M	1988
	540	1988
	720	1990
	70 B	1990
	200 DM	1990
1971	380	1988
	390	1989
	360	1990
1972	145	1988
1973	220	1988
	220	1990
1975	440	1988
	480	1989
	380	1990
1976	420	1987
	460	1990
1977	195	1989
1978	600 6M	1988
	540	1988
	600 6M	1988
	650	1990
1979	390	1988
	480	1990
1980	300	1989
1981	350	1988
	300	1989
1982	480 6M	1988
	480	1988
	500 6M	1989
	580	1990
1983	390 6M	1988
	500	1988
	420	1989
	480	1990
1984	180	1988
	230	1990
1985	420	1988
	420	1990
1986	520	1990

SOURCES

As I acknowledged in the introduction, this book could not have been written without M. René Pijassou's thesis on the Médoc, of which a shortened version was published in two volumes in September 1980 by Jules Tallandier.

The archives at Margaux consist only of:

1. Twenty-nine notarial minutes from the sixteenth century, showing land transactions by the then Sieurs de Margaux.

2. Twenty-seven notarial minutes dating between 1557 and 1619, relating to much smaller land transactions.

3. Two major land registers (*terriers*), one, of 348 pages, drawn up between 1684 and 1686 for Jean Denis d'Aulède. The other, which complements the earlier one, was drawn up between 1688 and 1692. There is also the document of the same period in which M. de Rauzan recognizes that he owes the Seigneur de Margaux rent of a *barrique* of wine.

4. Documents on the Revolutionary period, including the Inventory relating to the sale of the estate to Laure Fumel, the accounts of the lease from 1797 to 1802 and documents relating to the purchase of the château by Bertran Douat.

5. Table (*tableaux de récoltes*) of the vintages from 1795 to 1918 are on three large sheets of paper, preserved under glass.

6. Documents relating to the period 1920-35, when the estate was owned by the *Société Viticole de Château Margaux*.

Secondary sources which were useful included:

Feret's *Statistique Générale de la Gironde* Vol. III, which contains many valuable biographical details.
La Seigneurie et le Vignoble de Château Latour by Professor Charles Higounet and a group of scholars (who included M. Pijassou). This exhaustive study has a number of references to Margaux, and is also extremely useful for anyone trying to understand the geographical and geological factors involved in the making of great wine.
Guillon's *Les Châteaux Historiques et Vinicoles de la Gironde*, published in 1865, provides a resumé of the many myths which surround Château Margaux.
Successive editions of *Les Vins de Bordeaux*, published by Cocks and Feret, provide basic information on the size of the estate and its production from the 1840s to the present day.

But the greatest help and encouragement which any author on Bordeaux receives is from friends in the business. And in this respect I am particularly grateful not only to the late Monsieur Mentzelopoulos, Madame Mentzelopoulos and Corinne Mentzelopoulos, who gave me full run of the archive and the estate, and to their predecessors, Pierre and Bernard Ginestet, but also to the present *régisseur*, Philippe Barré, Paul Pontalier, his predecessor, the *maître de chai*, M. Jean Grangerou (and his father, Marcel Grangerou), to the *maître de culture*, Jean-Pierre Blanchard, and to everyone working at Margaux. Among the many others who helped me were M. René Zuger, M. Lucien Lurton, M. Daniel Lawton, M. Guy Schÿler, Madame Avisseau of the Archives Départmentales de la Gironde, Professor Pariset, M. Robert Coustet and Mr. Anthony Berry.

As always, the staffs at the Bodleian Library, the London Library and the Bibliothéque Municipale in Bordeaux were unfailingly helpful and courteous.

CHAPTER 1 THE FORTUNES OF MARGAUX

– The Pontacs and the English
'Sir Robert Walpole's Wine' in *Men and Places* by J. H. Plumb 1963.

James Brydges, First Duke of Chandos by C. H. C. and Muriel I. Baker.

– Margaux as a Major Agricultural Business
Communay *Le Parlement de Bordeaux* 1886, gives some information on the d'Aulède de Lestonnac family. M. Pigassou has transcribed the 'Mémoire' on wine-making, now in the possession of M. Nathaniel Johnston. The information on Madame d'Aulède's problems with the taxmen comes from document C3214 in the Archives Départmentales de la Gironde.

– The du Barry Connection
Information on the du Barry brothers from *The Guardian of Marie Antionette* by Lillian C. Smythe 1902.

Quotation from *Anecdotes sur Madame la Comtesse du Barri* by Pidansat de Mairobert 1775.

– The Revolution at Margaux
The basic information comes from the documents at the château, and from files number Q1755 and Q1769 at the Archives Départmentales. The information on Mathieu Miqueau comes from Marion and Benzecar *Documents Inédits sur l'Histoire Economique de la Révolution Française* 1912.

The Barton-Guestier-Johnston links are explained in *Fide et

SOURCES

Fortitudine by Cyril Ray (privately printed): Information on the profitability of the lease from information kindly supplied by M. Guy Schÿler.

Madame Duvigneau, of the Archives Municipales de Bordeaux, kindly traced for me the certificate of the ill-fated Brane-Fumel marriage.

– Colonilla – and the Estate he Bought
On Beltran Douat, see article by the Marques del Saltillo in the *Revista de Historia y de Genealogia Española* Secunda epoca Tome IV 1930. The inventory of the fomer house is preserved at the château: I am grateful to M. Robert Coustet for helping me to recreate the shape of the exterior from the inventory.

– A Bankable Proposition
For Aguado see entry in *Dictionnaire de Biographie Française.*

Maurice Healy *Claret and the White Wines of Bordeaux* Constable 1934.

For Madame Aguado *The Court of the Tuileries* by 'Le petit homme rouge'.

My Mistress, the Empress Eugénie by Madame Curette from *The Empress Eugénie 1870-1910* by Edward Legge, Harper & Bros. 1910.

On the *abonnement* see the archives of Tastet and Lawton.

On the price and profitability of estates see A. Charles *Le Commerce des Vins de Bordeaux sous le 2ème Empire*, in *Revue Historique de Bordeaux* 1962.

Apart from the works previously cited, there is some information on the Pillet-Wills in the draft contracts of the takeover from them, preserved at the château.

CHAPTER 3 THE RENAISSANCE OF MARGAUX

Most of the geological information comes from Professor Enjalbert's contribution to the *Seigneurie et Vignoble de Château Latour*. M. Seguin works at the Institut Viticole of The University of Bordeaux. Dr. Christopher Hawkesworth of the Open University helped translate and explain French geological terms for me.

CHAPTER 4 THE "VERSAILLES OF THE MEDOC"

Madame Gouyou of the University of Bordeaux has compiled a very useful bibliography of the available literature and extant drawings on and of Louis Combes. The key sources are three articles by Professor Pariset:

Les théories artistiques d'un architecte du neo-classicisme in Annales du Midi 1964.

Louis Combes in the Revue Historique de Bordeaux Vol. XXII, and *Château Margaux and the Architect Combes* in Vignobles et Vins d'Aquitaine 1970.

The Combes drawings are in the Fonds Delpit at the Bibliothèque Municipale de Bordeaux.

M. Philippe Maffre discovered Combes' abortive plans for Château Olivier.

CHAPTER 5 THE "BEAU IDEAL OF CLARET"

Jefferson and Wine. Vinifera Wine Growers Association, the Plains, Virginia.

The quote from M. Galos comes from the Archives of the Chambre de Commerce in Bordeaux.

Ian Maxwell Campbell was writing in *Wayward Tendrills of the Vine*. Chapman and Hall, London 1948.

William Lawton's *Memorandum* is preserved at the offices at Tastet et Lawton.

Cyrus Redding *A History and Description of Modern Wines* 1833.

Charles Cocks *Bordeaux, Its Wines and the Claret Country* Longman 1846.

H. Warner Allen *The Wines of France* and, later *Natural Red Wines* Constable 1951.

APPENDIXES

Vintage Notes
Dates of the vintage, weather and other notes transcribed from documents preserved at Margaux. Overall vintage assessments from Michael Broadbent's *Great Vintage Wine Book II*, Mitchell Beazley in association with Christie's Wine Publications 1991.

Prices at Auction
Christie's Wine Reviews and catalogue archives.

GLOSSARY

Abonnements (contracts): Fixed-term contracts between proprietors and groups of *négociants,* introduced in the mid-nineteenth century, whereby the merchants guaranteed to buy the next five or ten years' crops for a fixed price. They became increasingly popular in the early twentieth century.

Appellation (d'Origine) Contrôlée (AC or AOC): French designation guaranteeing the origin, production methods, alcoholic strength and quantity of the wine produced.

Assemblage: The blending of different "lots" of wine and grape varieties from the same *cru,* the aim being to ensure a single uniform wine.

Barrique: Standard Bordeaux barrel with a capacity of 225 litres, usually of oak, for ageing and sometimes shipping wine.

Chai (wine storeroom): Generally built above ground level; wine is stored here in barrels. However, some are underground in Bordeaux. They often house the estate's administrative offices.

Chartreuse: A .small château, long and low in shape, peculiar to the Bordeaux region.

Chef de Culture: In larger properties in Bordeaux the outdoors equivalent of the *maître de chai*; the foreman of the vineyard.

Claret: Adapted from the old French word, *clairet,* meaning a pale-red wine. The word is used in Britain to describe the red wines of Bordeaux.

Coulure: A pollination failure of the young vine. It manifests itself either by the withering of some of the flowers or grapes, or by their unequal growth.

Cru Classé (classed growth): Applied in particular to the 1855 classification of Médoc châteaux.

Cuve (vat): A large container, made of wood, stone, concrete or stainless steel, in which the wine is fermented.

Elevage: The nurturing and treatment of the wine between fermentation and bottling.

Grand Vin: Not a recognized or regulated term, but generally used to mean the first or selected wines of a property, in contrast to the second or other wines.

Jalles: A local term in Bordeaux for the small tributaries of the Garonne and the Gironde rivers or the drainage channels in the former marshland.

Oenologist: Anyone versed in oenology.

Oneology: The science of wine.

Oidium: Fungus disease similar to mildew that attacks the vine. Oidium ravaged the vineyards of Europe in the mid-nineteenth century. Can be treated with sulphur spray.

Ouillage: The replenishing of wine in the barrel lost due to evaporation.

Palus: Low, damp land on the banks of the Dordogne, the Garonne and the Gironde in the Bordeaux region.

Parlement: The local governing bodies in France from before the Revolution. In Bordeaux the *Parlement* was established in 1451. It was mainly an appeal court dealing with civil and criminal cases, but also had the power to protest against decrees issued by the King and central government.

Parlementaire: Member of the *Parlement.* Members were elected and benefits were social rather than financial. The *Parlementaires* lost their power during the French Revolution but even today the prestige of a Bordeaux family often stems from power originally incurred as members of the *Parlement.*

Phylloxera (*Phylloxera vastatrix*): An insect that attacks the *vinifera* roots. It arrived in Europe in the mid-nineteenth century, and in France in 1860 wreaking almost fatal damage to vineyards.

Pied de cuve: The best, carefully selected grapes which form the basis of the *grand vin.*

Pieds de vigne: The rootstock of individual vine plants.

Piquette: A thin, watery wine made from the pressings, which has been until very recently the usual beverage of the Médocain working classes.

Pourriture grise (Grey rot): Spoilage of grapes attacked by a fungus (*botrytis*) before they mature. This same fungus can have beneficial effects, see *purriture noble* (noble rot).

Quai des Chartrons: Central district of Bordeaux where activities connected with the wine trade have developed over the centuries and where the wine companies are traditionally based.

Régisseur (estate manager): The person responsible for the administration and organization of a vineyard.

Soutirage: The 'racking' of the wine from a barrel or vat once the gross less, or sediment have sunk to the bottom.

Terroir: Land, considered from the point of view of wine production.

Tonneau: The measure (900 litres) in which Bordeaux is still bought and sold from the château.

Vendange: Grape harvest.

Vignoble (vineyard): All the vines cultivated in a *cru,* an *appellation* or a region.

Vin de presse: Wine made from gentle pressing of the solid matter removed from the vats after fermentation.

INDEX

PHOTOGRAPHIC CREDITS